Tantra

THE FOUNDATION OF BUDDHIST THOUGHT SERIES

Tantra

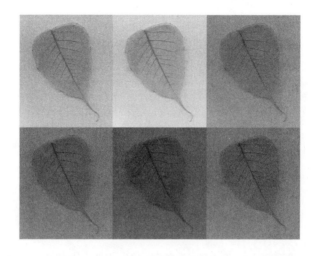

THE FOUNDATION of BUDDHIST THOUGHT

VOLUME 6

GESHE TASHI TSERING

FOREWORD BY LAMA ZOPA RINPOCHE

EDITED BY GORDON MCDOUGALL

WISDOM PUBLICATIONS • BOSTON

Wisdom Publications, Inc.
199 Elm Street
Somerville MA 02144 USA
www.wisdompubs.org

Library of Congress Cataloging-in-Publication Data

Tashi Tsering, Geshe, 1958–
Tantra / Geshe Tashi Tsering ; foreword by Lama Zopa Rinpoche ; edited by Gordon McDougall.
    pages cm. — (The foundation of Buddhist thought ; volume 6)
Includes bibliographical references and index.
ISBN 1-61429-011-3 (pbk. : alk. paper)
1. Tantric Buddhism. I. McDougall, Gordon, 1948– editor. II. Title.
BQ8915.4.T38 2012
294.3'925—dc23

                    2011048875

ISBN 978-1-61429-011-7
eBook ISBN 978-1-61429-012-4

16 15 14 13 12
5 4 3 2 1

Cover and interior design by Gopa&Ted2. Set in Goudy Oldstyle 10.5/16.

CONTENTS

LIST OF TABLES

Publisher's Acknowledgment

The publisher gratefully acknowledges the generous help of the Hershey Family Foundation in sponsoring the publication of this book.

FOREWORD

THE BUDDHA'S MESSAGE is universal. We all search for happiness but somehow fail to find it because we are looking for it in the wrong direction. Only when we start cherishing others will true happiness grow within us. And so the Buddha's essential teaching is one of compassion and ethics, combined with the wisdom that understands the nature of reality. The teachings of the Buddha contain everything needed to eliminate suffering and make life truly meaningful, and as such the teachings are not only relevant to today's world, but vital.

This is the message my precious teacher, Lama Thubten Yeshe, gave to his Western students. His vision to present the Dharma in a way that was accessible and relevant to everyone continues and grows as his legacy. His organization, the Foundation for the Preservation of the Mahayana Tradition (FPMT), now has centers all over the world, and Lama's work is carried on by many of his students.

The Foundation of Buddhist Thought, developed by Geshe Tashi Tsering, is one of the core courses of the FPMT's integrated education program. The essence of Tibetan Buddhist philosophy can be found within its curriculum, consisting of six different subjects in Buddhist thought and practice. *The Foundation of Buddhist Thought* serves as a wonderful basis for further study in Buddhism, as well as a tool to transform our everyday lives into something meaningful.

Geshe Tashi has been the resident teacher at Jamyang Buddhist Centre, London, since 1994. He has been incredibly beneficial in skillfully guiding the students both in London and in many other centers where he teaches. Besides his profound knowledge—he is a Lharampa Geshe, the highest educational qualification within our tradition— his excellent English and deep understanding of Western students means that he can present the Dharma in a way that is both accessible and relevant. His wisdom, compassion, and humor are combined with a genuine gift as a teacher. You will see within the six books of *The Foundation of Buddhist Thought* series the same combination of profound understanding and heart advice that can guide both beginner and experienced Dharma practitioner alike on the spiritual path.

Whether you read this book out of curiosity or as part of your spiritual journey, I sincerely hope that you find it beneficial and that it shows you a way to open your heart and develop your wisdom.

Lama Zopa Rinpoche
Spiritual Director
The Foundation for the Preservation of the Mahayana Tradition

PREFACE

I AM EXTREMELY HAPPY and more than a little amazed that this sixth and last book in the *Foundation of Buddhist Thought* (FBT) series has been finally completed. When Wisdom Publications first approached me to modify the existing course books into the stand-alone ones that now comprise the six volumes of the series, I was, to be quite frank, very reluctant, knowing that there were already many books published on the various subjects, written by great teachers and scholars with far more experience and understanding than I have.

However, I could see that to produce such books might be useful to many people. My aim was to produce a set of books that was neither very basic nor overly academic, books that would not be too long but still combine to give a comprehensive view of Buddhism, and particularly Tibetan Buddhism. I could also see how improving the existing course books would make the study experience of the students of the Foundation of Buddhist Thought richer. Over the years, a gratifying number of people had completed the course and seemed to have benefited from it. For those reasons, I overcame my initial reluctance. I was still, however, acutely aware of my lack of deep understanding and of my inability to clearly explain the subjects in a language that is my second language.

That is particularly true of this last book, on Buddhist tantra. To tackle such a profound and esoteric subject, and such a vast one, and to create an accessible, comprehensible book that didn't just gloss over the logic and mechanics of a Vajrayana practice, was in fact so daunting that I kept delaying and delaying rewriting this book. Some of you who have bought the other five books in this series may have wondered at the long delay between the previous books and this one. I was so nervous about getting the level of explanation and the details right that I almost told Wisdom Publications I could not do it. For almost three years I procrastinated, researching a little, rereading a section of what I had previously written and wondering how to alter it, and then putting it down again. Slowly, however, over that long period, with research in books and the advice of my teachers, I was able to overcome that reluctance. I must still apologize for any points that are unclear or inaccurate—and I am sure there are some—but I hope that this book will be of benefit to you nonetheless.

In the end, with the help of some of my great teachers, I decided to focus on two areas: an overview of the three lower classes of tantras and a reasonably detailed explanation of highest yoga tantra.

Chapter 1 is a brief introduction to the tantric tradition and includes a look at the vital prerequisites for tantric practice and the all-important concept of deity yoga. In chapter 2, we enter the world of tantra, with a look at the need for a strong student-teacher relationship and the initiation that is the starting point of any tantric practice.

In chapters 3 and 4, we explore the lower tantras, first looking at the difference between the tantras and then the levels we progress through if we practice a lower tantra. To illustrate that, we work through a very simple, but very beautiful, tantric practice from the first of the four classes, *kriya tantra*. Even though it is relatively simple, it is a very clear illustration of how tantra works.

The last four chapters deal exclusively with highest yoga tantra, the most complex and subtle of all the classes of tantra. Here, we will look

at the underlying psychology of this system of tantras as well as the subtle winds, or energies, that it employs to completely transform the
mind. We will also explore the way a practitioner learns how to use
ordinary death, intermediate state, and rebirth as a tool to develop on
the path, by mimicking the mental processes that occur at death within
a tantric practice.

I have tried to find a balance between pure theory and practical
explanation of what needs to be done in meditation, and I hope what
follows works whether you are reading this book out of mere curiosity
or you are actually engaging in a Vajrayana practice.

This reflects the overall ethos of the six *Foundation of Buddhist
Thought* books, which were specifically designed to lead somebody from
any Buddhist tradition with a basic understanding of the general topics within Buddhism to a deeper level, without being too complex.
While this last book, on tantra, is very much from a Tibetan Buddhist
perspective, I feel that the six books together form a reasonably complete picture of the Buddhist path, which, within the two-year correspondence or campus course that they were intended for, provides a
structured approach to the study of Buddhism.

Since I formulated this course in the late 1990s, a good number of
people have completed it, and I'm extremely pleased how it is con-
tinuing to draw people and how they seem to be getting something useful from it. But this course is not one person's effort. Many, many people
worked hard to make it available. Because this is the last book, I would
like to offer my deep appreciation to all the people who supported and
helped in both the running of the course and the creation of these
books. There are too many to name, but I would like to mention a few.

First and foremost I want to give sincere, genuine thanks, from the
bottom of my heart, to Kyabje Zopa Rinpoche. This course would not
exist without his support. There was one time when it seemed unlikely
the course would come to fruition, but Rinpoche's encouragement

really helped me persevere, and because of Rinpoche the Foundation of Buddhist Thought is now a core program in the FPMT (Foundation for the Preservation of the Mahayana Tradition) education curriculum. Because of his support, these books are now available, and this course still continues, so I deeply, sincerely thank him and wish him a long, long life and pray the apparent obstacles to his health may be soon overcome.

I would also like to thank my precious teacher, Geshe Thubten Rinchen. Since I joined Sera Monastery when I was thirteen years old, his support has been invaluable to me, not just the enormous number of teachings he gave me, but the day-to-day advice that guided my life. There are no words to express the kindness and the invaluable advice he has given me.

Then, of course, my late mother, Dolma, and my father, Jamyang. These two people brought me up when we became refugees, and under those circumstances they gave a hundred and ten percent of everything they had—their love, their energy, their kindness, their gentleness, their wisdom—to raise us eight siblings.

I must also thank Jamyang Buddhist Centre, London, where I have been a resident teacher since 1994. There are many people over the years who have given me support, both in general and specifically with this course: typing transcripts, rewriting material, recording the teachings, and administering and tutoring the course. I would like to especially thank Gordon McDougall. Patient, knowledgeable, with good understanding of my bad habits, Gordon is a really good friend who did all the hard work to bring these books to life. And I would also like to thank Wisdom Publications for their patience and generosity and especially David Kittelstrom, Wisdom's main editor. For their help and the many different ways they have supported me over the years, may I offer a huge thank you to everybody.

Finally, I sincerely hope this series of books will be beneficial to anybody who sincerely wants to study Buddhism. Whatever merit has been created since the inception of the course in creating it, teaching it, and doing whatever was needed to maintain and enhance it, I would like to dedicate to His Holiness the Dalai Lama. May he have a long, long life, and may all his projects and activities to bring peace, harmony, and tolerance to this world be successful and free from obstacles.

Thank you.

1 THE UNIQUENESS OF TANTRA

Sutra and Tantra

AFTER HIS ENLIGHTENMENT under the bodhi tree more than twenty-five hundred years ago, the historical Buddha, Shakyamuni, taught continuously for more than forty years to many different followers in many different places. All of the Buddha's teachings are without contradiction in that they all lead to freedom from suffering. Still, esoteric teachings like the Vajrayana practices can seem far removed from the more common ethical advice and meditation techniques of his other teachings.

Tibetan Buddhism is generally divided into three vehicles, or *yanas*: the individual liberation vehicle, the Hinayana; the universal liberation vehicle, the Mahayana; and the tantric vehicle, the Vajrayana. The practices and teaching of the first two vehicles, the Hinayana and Mahayana, are the foundation of Vajrayana practice. The main teachings of the Hinayana are the four noble truths, the thirty-seven aspects of enlightenment, and the twelve links of dependent origination.[1] In the Mahayana, the main teachings are the practices of the altruistic awakened mind (*bodhichitta*) and the trainings of the bodhisattva, such as the six perfections.[2] It is crucial that anybody interested in practicing tantra prepares by first thoroughly practicing the path laid out in the other two vehicles.

Hinayana practitioners can choose whether they incorporate teachings from the other two vehicles into their practice. For practitioners of the Mahayana, however, there is no choice—they must base their practice on a firm foundation in the Hinayana teachings. This becomes even more important for a practitioner of Vajrayana. This is not to say that there is a "superior" or "inferior" vehicle—which vehicle is best is determined by the disposition of each individual practitioner. But the later vehicles are built upon the wisdom and practice of the earlier ones; there is no shortcut. Thus I cannot emphasize enough how vital it is for a person entering the Vajrayana to be fully grounded in the teachings of the other two vehicles. To attempt tantric practice without the foundation of the four noble truths or a well-developed sense of altruism would be at best futile and at worst disastrous. It is important to see how Vajrayana fits into the whole of Buddhism so you don't make the mistake of seeing it as a separate and unconnected practice. The tantric tradition is rooted in all of the Buddha's teachings. Thus before you attempt to understand tantra, it is very important to have a basic understanding of the fundamentals of Tibetan Buddhism—from the other books in the Foundation of Buddhist Thought series or elsewhere.

Furthermore, it is important to note that Buddhist Vajrayana tantra is quite different from the tantra practiced in non-Buddhist Indian traditions. On the surface there are many similarities, but as you will see, Buddhist tantric practices are imbued with the realizations of the other two vehicles, making it quite distinct.

Tantra and the Mahayana

THE PREREQUISITES

The goals of Buddhist tantric practice are the elimination of all delusions, the cessation of all suffering, and the attainment of enlightenment. Its main objectives are the cultivation of an altruistic mind and a realization of the nature of reality. As such it is no different from any other Mahayana practice. The methods it employs, however, are quite different.

Vajrayana practices are incredibly powerful. Vajrayana is called the *resultant vehicle*, as opposed to the Sutrayana, which is called the *causal vehicle*. This is because in Vajrayana practice we imagine ourselves as we would like to be, as an enlightened being, and this enables us to actualize that state much more quickly. However, the quick development and power of the practice can be dangerous if done incorrectly, so our foundation must be firm before we can begin.

First and foremost, tantric practice requires *refuge*. Somebody with a genuine interest in Vajrayana practice requires a strong refuge in the Buddha, the Dharma, and the Sangha. This is true for any Buddhist practice.

Because Vajrayana practice belongs to the Mahayana tradition, we also need a good understanding of and feeling for *bodhichitta*, the mind that aspires to enlightenment in order to benefit all other beings. The compassionate mind of bodhichitta that cannot bear the suffering of others and strives to find the best way to eliminate it is the essence and core practice of the Mahayana. Without a mind utterly determined to do whatever is possible to free every other living being from suffering, our practice of Vajrayana cannot succeed.

Vajrayana practice is also impossible without a deep understanding of *emptiness*. During Vajrayana practice we are asked to visualize ourselves as a deity arising from emptiness. What does that mean? These visualizations are subtle and the understanding that underpins them profound. Without seeing these visualizations in the context of the emptiness of inherent existence, they are no more effective than a child imagining herself as a fairy. Only with a good understanding of emptiness will these practices make sense, and only when they make sense will we be able to gain any benefit from them.

The necessary prerequisites for a Vajrayana practice are therefore refuge, a strong yearning for the altruistic mind of bodhichitta, and a good intellectual understanding of emptiness. The greater these precious states are within our mindstream, the more powerful our Vajrayana practice will be; the more we advance in our Vajrayana practice, the more we will develop toward the true realization of bodhichitta and emptiness.

THE VAJRAYANA WAS TAUGHT BY THE BUDDHA

We can reasonably say that 2,550 years ago in Sarnath, India, the Buddha taught the essence of the four noble truths. Likewise we know the precise location and circumstances of many sutras, so we can imagine with relative accuracy the monastery, the shady trees, the disciples clustered around the Buddha, and the Buddha giving his discourse.

The origins of the Vajrayana teachings are not so easy to pin down. Not only were the place and time of the teachings very different from the other parts of the Buddhadharma but so was the aspect the Buddha took when he taught them. As an enlightened being, the Buddha had the ability to manifest in many aspects. During his forty years of teaching, he most commonly assumed the aspect of a monk in simple robes, leading his community of Sangha and going out among the laypeople to tell them about the Dharma. The aspect he chose for giving the Vajrayana teachings was more mystical.

There are said to be three bodies of a buddha: the *dharmakaya*, or truth body, the *sambhogakaya*, or enjoyment body, and the *nirmanakaya*, or emanation body. A buddha in the dharmakaya aspect, the essence of a buddha's inner realizations, is unable to communicate with other beings. In the sambhogakaya aspect, he or she is able to communicate with *arya* beings, those who have reached an exalted level of realization. Ordinary beings like us can't perceive a sambhogakaya, however, so a buddha must assume the nirmanakaya aspect to reach out to us, which is what the Buddha did during his time on earth. For the Vajrayana teachings, however, he assumed the sambhogakaya aspect, as did the beings who received the teachings.

The teachings of the Buddha preserved in Tibetan are collected in what is called the Kangyur. Of the just over one hundred volumes in the Kangyur, about a quarter are filled with texts on tantra. Most of these are brief ritual texts, and there are many hundreds of them. The link between the transmission of the tantras by the Buddha in the form of Vajradhara and us is the *mahasiddha*, a Sanskrit word meaning a tantric master with great (*maha*) attainments (*siddhi*). Each of the sadhanas and root tantras in the Kangyur was transmitted by a particular mahasiddha; there is a well-known enumeration of eighty-four such Indian mahasiddhas who lived around the end of the first millennium, the heyday of Buddhist tantra in India. A mahasiddha's disciples received the direct lineage of that tantra from him or her and then passed it on to their disciples, setting up an unbroken lineage that extends to us today. That means that the tantric empowerment or the commentary on the practice we receive comes in a lineage from the Buddha himself.

VAJRAYANA AND ITS MANY NAMES

Notice how I have used *Vajrayana* and *tantra* as synonyms. There are in fact several terms that refer to this same practice, each with a slightly different flavor. Although *tantra* is probably the most common term used for this practice, *Vajrayana* is perhaps clearer in that it avoids confusion with the Hindu tantra.

We don't generally translate *Vajrayana* into English, although some commentators call it the "diamond vehicle." In Tibetan it is *dorje tegpa*. *Dorje*, or the Sanskrit *vajra*, is a word that comes up frequently in

Mahayana Buddhism. There is no exact English translation. Although it is sometimes used as a noun to describe the five-spoked implement used with the bell in Vajrayana practices, in this case it is used as an adjective to mean "indestructible" or "inseparable." "Adamantine" is probably as good a translation as any, although I prefer "inseparable," with its connotation of emptiness and the mind realizing emptiness being one.

Tegpa, or the Sanskrit *yana*, means "vehicle" or "path." It is a "vehicle" in the sense of being that which carries us from one place to another—*tegpa* literally means "to support"—and a "path" in the sense of being the route we follow—in this case, to enlightenment.

Therefore Vajrayana can be defined as "the inseparable vehicle that will take us to our destination." In this practice, the two wings of Buddhism, method (or compassion) and wisdom (or emptiness), are practiced together, inseparably, within one single mental state. Both are practiced in the Sutrayana, too, but only in alternation; they cannot be practiced simultaneously within one mental state. As we will see later, this is why Vajrayana is such an expedient means to enlightenment— it brings bodhichitta and the wisdom realizing emptiness together in an entirely unique way.

The second name often used is *Mantrayana*. Again, *yana* tells us it is a vehicle or path. *Manas* means "mind" or "think," and the suffix *tra* means "to protect," so a *mantra* is something that protects the mind. Hence Mantrayana means "the vehicle that protects the mind."

There are many different ways to protect our mind, but here we are referring to protecting our mind from the sense of our own ordinariness. One of the most damaging concepts that we live with all the time, carrying it around like a huge weight, is the feeling that we are nothing special, that we are an impure being with an impure nature. In modern psychological terms, we might call this "baggage." We have all seen people who are crippled by a low sense of self-worth. Even if we are not like that ourselves, our own sense of limitation still blocks us from achieving our true potential. "I can't do that" is our mantra. The Mantrayana kind of mantra protects us from that defeating ordinariness.

The great teacher Lama Yeshe says:

> Our problem is that inside us there is a mind going, "Impossible, impossible, impossible. I can't, I can't, I can't." We have to banish that mind from this solar system. Anything is possible. Sometimes you feel that your dreams are impossible, but they are not. Human beings have great potential; they can do anything. The power of the mind is incredible, limitless.[3]

Through meditation on emptiness and bodhichitta, we use the visualization of arising as the enlightened deity to eliminate this sense of ordinariness. The practice of generating ourselves as the deity and holding a sense of what is called *divine pride* or *divine identity* is an integral part of Vajrayana practice. It is a way to bring the result into the practice by feeling that we are already what we will one day be. Generating this vision of ourselves as the deity with all of the deity's attributes can eliminate any sense that we do not have those qualities and can purify our delusions of inadequacy. By using our meditation practice to embody the final destination now, we create the causes to achieve that destination. This is the vehicle that protects our mind from ordinariness, Mantrayana.

Vajrayana is also called the *secret vehicle*. Its practices are incredibly subtle; they require a deep and experiential understanding that can only come from the initiation and instructions of a fully qualified spiritual teacher. To read randomly and idly about Vajrayana can lead to misconceptions. Western scholars' early labeling of Tibetan Buddhism as "Lamaism" is an example of this, as if Tibetan Buddhism were the cult of the lama.

It is strongly stated in the Vajrayana teachings that tantra should not be revealed to those who are not ready and that people who practice Vajrayana should do so privately and without showing their practice or the things they use for their practice to anybody else. It has been the tradition to not explain even the theory of Vajrayana to non-initiates, since any misinterpretation could weaken the lineage of the teachings. These days, however, many books about Vajrayana are available, and His Holiness the Dalai Lama has explicitly stated that there is no problem as long as the motivation for teaching or writing about Vajrayana is positive. Although in recent years this practice has begun to change, the tradition is still shrouded in more secrecy than perhaps any other Buddhist teachings.

Vajrayana is also sometimes known as the *resultant vehicle*. We are not yet enlightened, and although the environment we live in might be nice, I doubt if many of us consider it a celestial mansion. In Vajrayana, we bring the end results of the vehicle into the present; we become the enlightened being with all the enlightened qualities, and our environment—our *mandala*—becomes the divine environment.

Sutrayana is called the *causal vehicle* because it works on creating the causes for enlightenment. We want bodhichitta, so we start with our small compassion and develop it slowly until we achieve the precious bodhichitta. We want the wisdom realizing emptiness, so we take our small understanding and develop it to its fullest. In Vajrayana, we are both creating the causes and bringing those resultant aspects into the path. This strong belief in our buddha nature, our divine identity, has the power to destroy that sense of ordinariness incredibly quickly.

Finally, Vajrayana is also called the *method vehicle*. The Sutrayana and Vajrayana vehicles produce the same result, but their methods for achieving these goals are distinct. In the causal, or perfection, vehicle, we develop each of the six perfections, the sixth of which is wisdom, or the realization of emptiness. Each practice is extremely helpful in developing our mind along the path to enlightenment, but none has the power to bring us to enlightenment in and of itself. In Vajrayana, however, since we arise out of emptiness as the deity and then perform the divine activities of the deity, both method and wisdom are developed simultaneously. This gives us the chance to advance incredibly quickly.

Each of us has many subtle layers of body and mind; this subtle physiology is the site of many of tantra's unique methods. The subtle body consists of drops or essences (Skt. *bindu*; Tib. *tig-le*); psychic energies called *winds* (Skt. *vayu*; Tib. *lung*); energy channels (Skt. *nadi*; Tib. *tsa*); and areas where those channels concentrate, called *chakras*, such as at the crown, the throat, and the center of the chest. The manipulation of these subtle energies to attain bodhichitta and realize emptiness is a central feature of Vajrayana practice. This special methodology is only found in Vajrayana, hence the name *method vehicle*.

Although Vajrayana is known by many different names, they all serve to reference the same unique and expedient means that characterize this practice.

The Unique Features of Vajrayana

As we have just seen, Vajrayana and the causal perfection vehicle share a single goal—full enlightenment—but their methods differ. In order to understand the defining characteristics of Vajrayana, let us first look at the similarities between Vajrayana and Sutrayana practice. It is said that both vehicles are the same in five ways:

+ attainment
+ bodhichitta
+ the six perfections
+ view
+ intention

The *attainment*, or result, of both vehicles is identical. Both lead to enlightenment, so neither vehicle is inferior in this respect.

The mind of enlightenment, *bodhichitta*, is also identical in both vehicles. There are two levels of bodhichitta—*aspiring bodhicitta*, the genuine, uncontrived aspiration to attain enlightenment that nevertheless lacks the power to actually perform a bodhisattva's activities, and *engaged bodhichitta*, where the mind is purified enough to spontaneously and continuously develop the six perfections. Engaged bodhichitta can be actualized in the practice of either vehicle; when we attain bodhichitta in Vajrayana, it is exactly the same as in Sutrayana.

Likewise, the *six perfections*—generosity, patience, morality, joyous perseverance, concentration, and wisdom—are perfections whether they are achieved through Vajrayana or Sutrayana practice.

The *view* is the wisdom realizing emptiness, the final mode of existence of things and events. There is no difference between the emptiness we realize as Sutrayana practitioners and the emptiness we realize as Vajrayana practitioners.

Finally, there is no difference in the *intention* of the practice. A Sutrayana practitioner's motivation is to attain enlightenment in order to be able to free all sentient beings from suffering. A Vajrayana practitioner's motivation is exactly the same. Both aim to benefit all living beings without exception and without discrimination. This is what defines both Sutrayana and Vajrayana as Mahayana practices. If one vehicle had a lesser intention, it would not be Mahayana.

THE FOUR COMPLETE PURITIES

As we have seen, although the results of the two vehicles might be identical, the methods are quite different, and this is what makes Vajrayana both unique and extremely powerful. In Vajrayana practice we develop divine pride, where we feel we really are the deity we are practicing, which cuts through our ordinary appearances. We can understand the elements of this unique deity practice through what are called the *four complete purities*. They are:

+ the complete purity of environment
+ the complete purity of body
+ the complete purity of resources
+ the complete purity of activities

The first is the *complete purity of environment*. In most Vajrayana meditation manuals, or *sadhanas*, there is a section where practitioners are instructed to visualize the environment of the deity, called the *mandala* or *celestial mansion*. These visualizations are often quite elaborate, with many attendant deities and structures. We are asked to imagine the mandala in such a way that we feel that it is our present reality, with us here and now. This is part of losing the sense of ordinariness. At present we see the places where we live and work as ordinary, with good and bad features. By purifying into emptiness and then visualizing our environment as perfect, we are bringing the result into the present by feeling we are already a buddha in a buddha's perfect environment.

In the same way, the *complete purity of body* is not our current impure body but the pure body of the deity that arises out of emptiness. Just as the house we live in, on this noisy street, with its dirty windows and broken door, is transformed into the divine residence of the deity, so the sense we hold of this body, with its pains and imperfections, is dissolved into emptiness. And from that emptiness we visualize ourselves arising as the body of the deity.

It is not as if we slip a deity body on top of this imperfect body like some rubber suit; we actually feel that we are the deity and our body is the divine body of the deity. With this level of identification with the deity, we have the power to completely purify our sense of ordinariness.

Where the Sutrayana chips away at our delusions, here we blast them into nonexistence with the power of our pure visualizations.

Likewise we see all the objects around us as pure in the *complete purity of resources*. In every Vajrayana practice, we as the deity make offerings of flowers, incense, light, and so forth to the deity. These are ordinary objects, but we do not offer ordinary objects to the deity. We must see these offering objects as divine objects and the action of offering as a divine action.

Thus the resources we use while we are doing Vajrayana practice are transformed into pure substances. Everything we eat, drink, or wear; everything we feel or sense; everything our mind comes into contact with is seen not as an ordinary object of the senses but as divine. Seeing everything that arises to our consciousness as extraordinary develops our potential to experience joy or bliss. This meditative bliss is far greater than any bliss we could experience in ordinary life through encountering the everyday pleasant objects of the senses.

Finally there is the *complete purity of activities*. During Vajrayana practice, the sadhana will instruct us to do many things to benefit sentient beings. These are the pure activities of that deity, and as we have visualized ourselves as that deity, these are also our activities. In Sutrayana we practice generosity, but the generosity practiced in Vajrayana can be far more extensive, because it is not an ordinary human but the deity giving things—food, money, teachings, and so forth—to all sentient beings. Whatever we do, we try to experience as divine. None of our actions retains the least trace of ordinariness; this is why it is called the *complete purity of activities*.

Vajrayana Combines Method and Wisdom

In both Sutrayana and Vajrayana, the method side and the wisdom side of the practice must be fully developed to attain enlightenment. Sutrayana practices can combine these two aspects but not, as in

Vajrayana, in one mind, and so both are developed at different times using different types of mind, the emotional side of our mind bringing about a deeper and deeper compassion and the rational side bringing about a more profound understanding of reality.

We have already seen that there are three bodies of a buddha, but in fact there are various ways of designating how a buddha can manifest. The sambhogakaya and nirmanakaya of a buddha are aspects of the form body (Skt. *rupakaya*), and so a more elemental way of looking at this is to divide the enlightened aspects into two: the truth body and the form body—the dharmakaya and rupakaya. The dharmakaya is mainly the nature of a buddha's mind, and the rupakaya is a buddha's form and vast activities.

This neatly links with the two sides of the practice, method and wisdom, and the two truths that must be realized, relative truth and ultimate truth. Relative or conventional truth is that which is true to a valid conventional consciousness. It is the world as we see it, when we are not analyzing how things actually exist, which is ultimate truth, the understanding of emptiness.

The great pandit Nagarjuna, in his *Precious Garland* (*Ratnavali*), shows how the two truths are the bases for the two bodies of the buddha, where the base of conventional truth is the method side of the path leading to the rupakaya, and the base of ultimate truth is the wisdom side of the path leading to the dharmakaya. Similarly, as humans, our interactions with one another are driven by two basic components: emotions and rational thought. Our emotions can be likened to the method side based on conventional understanding, while rational thought can be likened to the wisdom side based on an understanding of how things truly exist. When we become enlightened, these two aspects form the two bodies of the buddha we have become. To attain full enlightenment, these two causes must be accumulated equally—realizing emptiness will not take us all the way, nor will realizing bodhichitta. Sutrayana sees these practices as distinct.

Of course, during the path, these two minds do support each other. For instance, meditating on emptiness just before practicing generosity or ethics makes those practices more effective. They are supported by, or conjoined with, the wisdom realizing emptiness, but they are not the wisdom realizing emptiness itself. And it is the same the other way around—if we engage in extensive practices of generosity or ethics, our meditation on emptiness will become far more powerful. Generally speaking, however, the two minds remain distinct in the Sutrayana. In the Vajrayana, by contrast, by arising as the deity out of emptiness, whatever activities we do—the method side of the practice—are combined with the understanding of emptiness. Thus both method and wisdom are developed simultaneously, making our development very rapid indeed if we do the practice purely.

In Sutrayana, the cultivation of bodhichitta and the first five of the six perfections are cooperative conditions rather than direct causes of eventually achieving the rupakaya. In Vajrayana, on the other hand, methods such as utilizing the subtle body, the subtle winds, and the subtle mind within the practice of the visualization of the deity—based on a strong understanding of emptiness and bodhichitta—are direct causes of the rupakaya.

In other words, the causes and conditions we create by practicing the four complete purities are the direct causes and conditions of the rupakaya. This is the power of the resultant vehicle, of bringing the result into the present. This is why the Vajrayana path is thought of as a quicker way to enlightenment.

Deity Yoga

PRACTICING DEITY YOGA

The principal technique used in Vajrayana is visualizing a deity, either in front of us in *front-generation*, or visualizing ourselves as the deity in *self-generation.* With this method we are able to practice the four complete purities and conjoin method and wisdom within the subtlest mind. This is called *deity yoga.*

There are various prerequisites for the practice of deity yoga. At the physical level, we need to be human. In Vajrayana terms, that means we need to have subtle channels running through our body, along which the mind travels riding on the wind energies. In our normal daily existence, two faculties are necessary to experience the universe we live in. One is the ability to know. Thus we require a mind, since *mind* in Buddhism is defined as "that which is clear and knowing." The other is the ability of the mind to move to its object; that is the function of the wind energies. We also need the chakras—the concentrations of these channels at various points in our body—and the drops, which encompass the subtlest mind and winds. These are vital attributes needed in any tantric practice and particularly in the final part of highest yoga tantra, the most subtle of the Vajrayana systems of practice. We will discuss this in further detail when we look at highest yoga tantra in the later chapters of the book.

Although non-Buddhist tantric teachings and practices use similar visualizations of channels, winds, chakras, and drops to cultivate concentration and other achievements, in Vajrayana these practices are taken one step further and used to actualize bodhichitta and emptiness in the swiftest possible time. We are very fortunate to possess the physical requisites for the Vajrayana meditations. Over time, the visualizations become easier, our concentration increases, and we become more adept at utilizing the wind energies in our body, manipulating them so they aid our practice.

As we have just learned, in deity yoga we see ourselves as the deity and our environment, resources, and activities as pure. But what is a deity? The word has many connotations, which can cause confusion. The specific Tibetan term for a meditational deity is *yidam* (Skt. *ishtadevata*); deity yoga is called *lhayi neljor. Neljor* means "yoga," and the "yi" of *lhayi* refers to *yidam*. Therefore, in this instance, the *lha* of *lhayi* means an enlightened being. But outside of the context of deity yoga, *lha* (Skt. *deva*) may not necessarily refer to an enlightened being. It could just be a denizen of one of the god realms or a Hindu god.

Enlightened beings manifest in different aspects to best benefit sentient beings. The historical Buddha, Shakyamuni, manifested as an ordinary monk in order to establish the Dharma and the community of Sangha. It is a different manifestation of enlightened beings, however, that we call *deities*. There are many deities in Tibetan Buddhism: Tara, Avalokiteshvara, Vajrasattva, and so forth. These deities are enlightened beings, but it is mistaken to feel that they, like Shakyamuni, were once people who sat under a bodhi tree and attained enlightenment. Rather, they are manifestations of a particular enlightened energy. Individual beings attain enlightenment through practicing an attitude such as compassion. Their enlightened minds then manifest into an Avalokiteshvara aspect or a Tara aspect. For instance, the compassionate-action aspect of an enlightened being manifests as Tara. Avalokiteshvara is the buddhas' compassion.

Thus a deity may or may not be an enlightened being, and an enlightened being may or may not be a deity. The two categories overlap, but they are not identical. Thousands of beings have become enlightened in the same way Shakyamuni was, but it is inaccurate to call them deities. However, as enlightened beings they can manifest as a deity.

Since Tibetan Vajrayana employs many meditational deities whose function is to generate a specific energy determined by our particular propensities, some of us need to focus on a light, blissful energy, while others may be more suited to a forceful one. Just as sentient beings are diverse, we find a great variety of meditational deities in Tibetan Buddhism—peaceful and wrathful, alone or in union with a consort, with one head and two arms or with many heads, arms, and even legs.

Each of these features and attributes are rich with significance for the practitioner.

In Buddhist tantra, you often hear references to Vajradhara (Tib. *Dorje Chang*), either as the aspect the historical Buddha assumed to teach the tantras to the bodhisattvas, or as the primordial buddha. In some respects, all the other buddhas manifest from Vajradhara in the same way that the various enlightened energies arise from the fundamental state of enlightenment. As we will see when we look at vajra repetition in highest yoga tantra in the later chapters, although the meditations we are doing lead us to the state of Guhyasamaja (in the examples we will explore), at certain stages in the practice we arise as this primordial buddha, Vajradhara. Achieving the state of Vajradhara is synonymous with gaining all realizations and attaining buddhahood.

THE THREE ASPECTS OF DEITY YOGA

There are four classes of tantra, ascending in subtlety and complexity from kriya tantra to highest yoga tantra. Each class has its unique features, but three aspects of deity yoga are common to all Vajrayana practices:

+ divine identity
+ clarity
+ profundity

Divine identity or *divine pride* (Tib. *lhai ngagyal*) literally means "the self-identity of being a deity." As we have just seen with the four complete purities, an important feature of Vajrayana is the way the practice of visualizing ourselves as a deity can break us free from our sense of ordinariness. The goal is not to merely superimpose a deity form onto our ordinary, everyday self but to have the strong sense that we are indeed the deity. The stronger and clearer our identification with the deity is, the more effective our practice will be. It cannot work if it is a mere overlay on a persistent sense of ordinariness and inadequacy.

This concept might sound strange, but in fact we do it all the time—we take on roles and become them. Imagine you are training to be a teacher. When you first enter the classroom it feels a bit strange, but within a few years you *are* a teacher. When you are in front of a class, that is your persona. In Vajrayana we take it one step further. We let go of the mundane self-identity we carry around with us all the time, and when we lose that ordinary self, with all its faults and peculiarities, the space arises for us to acquire the persona of a deity with all the divine qualities.

This can only happen from the base of emptiness. Again, that is not as esoteric as it sounds. If we have no feeling for the mutability of the mind, then we will always be stuck in this mundane aspect of "me." But by understanding that there is nothing fixed or intrinsic in the mind, the self, the body, or any other part of ourselves, we suddenly have the freedom to change whatever aspects of ourselves we want to. That is the incredible freedom that emptiness brings—and if we can be anything, why not be enlightened?

This is not something that happens immediately. At first the practice can seem like an ill-fitting suit. But if we train ourselves again and again, we will start to see a profound change, not just during a meditation session but in how we relate to ourselves and to the external world. With divine pride, we can see our environment, and all living beings with it, as divine.

The second common element of deity yoga is *clarity* (Tib. *selnang*). *Clarity* here means the crispness and lucidity of our visualization. In the more advanced tantras such as highest yoga tantra, the visualizations become very elaborate. We need to develop this skill in order to progress in our meditation sessions. Without a clear visualization, our divine identity can never be that strong.

The last aspect of deity yoga common to all the tantras is *profundity* (Tib. *zabpa*). The visualization of the front- or self-generation deity in deity yoga is profound. It is more than an imagined picture in our head. It is more than an image that we label "me": "This is the deity with green skin and two arms, and this deity is me." It is much more than that, because we arise as the deity out of emptiness. This is so vital. In any sadhana we use to do a Vajrayana practice, just before the visualization we meditate on emptiness. Then, with a deep understanding of emptiness and having dissolved our ordinary appearance into emptiness, the deity that is us arises. This is how it is described—*tongpa ngenle*, "From emptiness the deity arises."

"From emptiness" does not mean that emptiness is like some kind of pot, and from that pot the deity appears. From a deep understanding of emptiness, an understanding of the mind itself arises. It is as if the self and the common concepts that pervade our whole experience dissolve, leaving a profound and blissful space. Within that space, within that sphere of understanding, the deity is visualized, either as front- or self-generation. The self is gone completely, the ordinariness is gone completely, and from the emptiness arises the deity.

That means that the deity has arisen from the fundamental nature of our mind, that ultimate subtle mind that is empty of inherent existence. Tara, or whichever deity we are visualizing, is not separate from our mind. She is not something outside us that we are evoking or inviting in, nor is she newly arisen from nowhere. She is our own fundamental nature manifesting in that way. Tara is the manifestation of the buddhas' activities, and by visualizing ourselves as Tara arising out of emptiness, we are creating the causes for us to have Tara's qualities ourselves.

Using profundity and clarity to generate divine pride, we visualize ourselves as the deity as powerfully as possible. We must combine this with emptiness, which takes understanding and determination. Only then do the environment, resources, and activities of the deity arise. This is the base upon which the whole of Vajrayana practice is founded. Without this strong and clear visualization, the rest of the practice—mantra recitation, offerings, and so forth—will be far less effective.

Utilizing Afflictive Emotions on the Path

Another unique feature of Vajrayana practice is how afflictive emotions (Skt. *klesha*) may be used on the path. One of the goals of any Buddhist path to enlightenment is the complete cessation of all deluded minds. In that, Vajrayana is no different from the other vehicles. But in Sutrayana an afflictive emotion such as anger or jealousy is seen as a stumbling block, and various antidotes are used to eliminate it, while in Vajrayana, those emotions can instead be used to aid in the path.

Attachment is almost always seen as a negative affliction in Sutrayana. One exception is for a bodhisattva, who must have some degree of attachment to his or her body in order to stay within this world system to help sentient beings. The analogy the Buddha used is manure: it is dirty and smelly and almost nobody wants it, but it is very useful for a farmer to grow crops. In the same way, attachment is dangerous and painful and seems like something we do not want. But bodhisattvas need to be reborn in samsara again and again to benefit sentient beings, so attachment to a body is useful for them.

Generally speaking, of course, the ordinary attachment of non-bodhisattvas—anger, pride, and so forth—must be eliminated whenever we encounter them. That is the Sutrayana view and the mainstream teaching of the Buddha. Such ordinary afflictive emotions are the source of all problems in the world. Vajrayana, however, employs a method where the energy of those afflictive emotions can be taken and molded into a creative energy that can actually help us. This is what "utilizing the afflictive emotions on the path" means. Many great teachers have written books on this subject, including Lama Yeshe's wonderful *Introduction to Tantra*, so I will only summarize the method here. Using attachment, anger, jealousy, and the other deluded minds on the path does not mean we become a deity full of attachment, anger, or jealousy. Far from it. Rather, we harvest the powerful energies that underlie those deluded minds in the service of the practice.

We can understand this profound technique using the example of anger. Think of a time when you were really furious with somebody. The emotion itself is terrible, with its conceptual justification and its subject—you as the harmed being—and its object—the harmer. Were we to simply accept the picture of reality that it paints, we would create problems for ourselves and others. But think of the power you have. It's like another being takes you over. It is that strong energy that manifests as shouting and red-faced fury. Strip the situation of everything but that energy, and you're left with something profound.

Here again, emptiness is the crucial factor. We go into the situation that made us angry, and then we meditate on emptiness while in that situation. Our understanding of emptiness will stop the anger but not the energy. We then bring that energy into the process of visualization.

This is more profound than doing a meditation on developing compassion and love for an enemy. There we are trying to destroy the anger by replacing it with its antidote, love. Such a practice can be effective with or without an understanding of emptiness. But with an understanding of emptiness, rather than eliminating the anger and its energy, we can transform it into something powerful.

That is not to say that we should go out looking for afflictive emotions. If we don't have any, that is wonderful; we can do the practice as it is meant to be done. But unfortunately we often come into a meditation session with something bubbling in our mind. Vajrayana gives us a skillful way of dealing with it. Rather than stopping the practice and going on to a meditation that brings in the antidote, we take that deluded mind and use it as fuel for deity yoga.

We can understand this practice using the analogy of insects born from wood. It is said that some insects are born from wood and that, after their birth, they eat the same wood from which they were born. In the same way, we can say that within the practice we are "born from the anger," and we use the energy of the anger to burn up that anger. A modern equivalent is vaccination—the raw material of the vaccination is the same as the disease it is curing.

The four classes of Vajrayana are described based on how much afflictive emotion the practitioner can utilize on the path. Some of us might be able to deal with a tiny amount of attachment, say to a chocolate bar, without being overwhelmed, but faced with a strong attachment, we would be lost. A practitioner of the highest class of Vajrayana is able to use very strong attachment to turn that energy into a profound practice.

To understand these ascending levels of practice, think of attraction to a sexual partner. It is said that in the first level of Vajrayana, kriya tantra, the practitioner can use the energy equivalent to seeing an attractive sexual partner; in charya tantra, he or she can use the energy equivalent to flirting with that person; and in yoga tantra, with touching each other. With highest yoga tantra, the practitioner must be able to use the energy of an actual sexual encounter on the path. That means that he or she can take the energy and use it without being overwhelmed by attachment to the partner or the act. I suspect not many of us are ready for that just yet.

2 ENTERING THE VAJRAYANA

The Door to the Vajrayana

THERE ARE MANY PATHS that lead us to a taking on a Vajrayana practice. Perhaps we have read an inspiring book by a great master or done a weekend meditation course at a local Buddhist center. Perhaps we have carefully studied the sutras and commentaries for years and now want to put that knowledge into practice in our daily lives. Sooner or later, many of us see that within the many deity practices in Vajrayana there is a very powerful and profound method to transform our minds.

Once we have developed a strong foundation of bodhichitta and a correct understanding of emptiness, the starting point of Vajrayana practice—the door we must pass through—is the initiation. Many Tibetan masters give tantric initiations in the West, which is wonderful, but there is really very little that can prepare us for this new world we are about to enter, with its cryptic language and foreign rituals. It does, however, help to read a book such as this, to gain some appreciation of the incredible and utterly relevant psychology that underpins all Vajrayana practices.

Which deity you practice depends on many factors. Hopefully, you will choose carefully, accepting the advice of your teacher, and end up taking an initiation into and doing the practice of the deity that most suits your disposition and that can most help you advance on your spiritual journey. Different vajra masters give different commitments when they give initiations—such as doing the full sadhana every day—and while this should not be the determining factor, you should consider whether you have the time and energy to follow such a practice. Perhaps a wrathful highest yoga tantra deity with many arms and faces is attractive to you, but is that the best practice for you to do? There are many considerations, and I recommend you discuss this fully with your fellow Dharma practitioners and especially with your teacher before you commit to one particular deity.

There are various forms and levels of initiation, including some that are extremely esoteric and rarified. I will focus on the most common ones. Most of us who want to begin Vajrayana practice will receive an initiation from a living being known as a *vajra master*. We must understand the significance of the vajra master, the role he or she plays in the initiation, and our relationship with him or her in order to truly progress on the path.

The Vajra Master and the Vajra Disciple

No matter what level of practice or type of Buddhism we undertake, we need a teacher to guide us. We can learn a few things from books, but to make true progress we need to have a relationship with a teacher who knows our propensities and can guide us skillfully.

Sometimes the way Tibetan Buddhism is written about in the West assumes that the student's level of involvement with the teacher is the same in all paths. But the method for teaching Mahayana is different from that used for teaching the subjects of the Hinayana path, and the difference in methodology becomes even more marked with Vajrayana, where there are unique and very important considerations that form a vital part of the practice that are not present in the other two paths. These very different paths seem to become conflated in books, so it is often unclear how vital the teacher-student relationship is to Vajrayana.

Within Tibetan Buddhism, the teacher-student relationship is almost always discussed in the context of a Vajrayana relationship, so it is often assumed that what applies to Vajrayana applies to the other vehicles as well. That is not true at all. In Vajrayana, a student is asked to do strict mind training on how to relate to the teacher; this is not true of the other paths. We will not examine those other paths here, but it is important to be aware of this distinction whenever you listen to a lama giving teachings on general Buddhist subjects like the four noble truths or karma.

Just because we receive teachings from somebody does not necessarily mean we should treat that person as our teacher—as our guru or lama. He or she can be seen as a spiritual friend giving a teaching in order to help us. We should have a deep respect for the teacher and the teachings, a strong awareness of the kindness of the teacher, and a strong conviction to follow the advice of the teacher as best as we are able, but the relationship need not go further than that. In the other paths it is certainly possible that teacher and student develop the closer guru-disciple relationship, but that is neither sure to happen nor a problem if it does not.

Many great Indian and Tibetan teachers have laid out the Buddhist path in a structured way in order to most skillfully lead practitioners from the very beginning all the way to enlightenment. In the Gelug tradition of Tibetan Buddhism, this is called the *lamrim*, the "graduated path to enlightenment." First formulated by the great scholar Atisha in his *Lamp for the Path* (*Bodhipathapradipa*), these lamrim teachings take the student from the most fundamental teachings on the four noble truths to the cultivation of bodhichitta and the realization of emptiness. With clear guidance on how to start on the path and proceed in the way that suits our particular disposition, we can make the best possible progress.[4]

Some of these lamrim texts emphasize the importance of finding the right teacher, establishing and keeping a pure relationship with him or her, and following his or her advice. Such explanations, although placed at the beginning of the text, are actually intended for a person preparing to become a tantric practitioner.

When we are ready to enter Vajrayana, these elements—finding the right teacher and maintaining a pure relationship based on seeing the teacher as pure—become vital. Although the basic structure is the same—a sense of conviction and deep respect, the ability to see the teacher's great qualities and recall his or her kindness, and so forth—the relationship to the teacher giving the tantric initiations and instructions is quite different from any we have had before.

This relationship is summed up beautifully in the verses of the *Guru Puja* (Tib. *Lama Chöpa*):

> You have the ten sets of qualities suitable for one
> To teach the path of those gone to bliss.
> Lord of Dharma, representing all conquerors,
> Mahayana guru, I make requests to you.
>
> You are wise, patient, honest,
> Without pretense or guile, your three doors well subdued.
> You have both sets of ten qualities, know tantra and rituals,
>   and are skilled in drawing and explaining:
> Foremost vajra holder, I make requests to you.[5]

We are asked to create a specific relationship with the teacher in order for the practice to be most fruitful. We need to see the person giving the initiation or the tantric teachings as our teacher, and likewise the teacher needs to accept that role and see us as his or her disciple. This kind of mutual acceptance is established on a thorough understanding of each other and of the teachings given and received.

When that acceptance has been established and we have received the initiation or teachings, that person becomes our teacher or guru, and we become that person's student or disciple.

In addition, within the context of our Vajrayana practice, we are asked to see our teacher as a buddha, a completely enlightened being. It is part of our practice and commitment to perceive our teacher as one with the enlightened deity of the particular tantric practice we undertake. This is a vital element of our practice, without which it would be ineffectual. There is no such instruction in the teachings of the other paths. When such a relationship is formed in the context of an initiation, the teacher giving the initiation becomes the vajra master, and the student becomes the vajra disciple. Both master and disciple now hold great responsibility.

There are ten qualities a vajra master must have and ten a vajra disciple must have. Ashvaghosha's *Fifty Verses on the Guru* (*Gurupanchashika*) describes the vajra master's qualities as:

> Reliable, disciplined, and intelligent,
> Patient, straightforward, and without deceit,
> Knowing the application of mantra and tantra,
> Compassionate, an expert in the explanatory texts,
> Learned in the ten categories
> And skilled in drawing the mandala,
> The master must have a full understanding of the mantra,
> Be full of faith, and have his senses under control.[6]

The vajra master needs to show great compassion toward the disciple and be inwardly disciplined. He or she must also know the sequences of the rituals of the initiation. If there is a mistake in the sequence, the initiation has not actually been given or received, and there will be great risk in doing the practice as if it had.

A master who is giving a highest yoga tantra initiation must have done a long retreat on that particular deity with a great fire puja at the end. He or she must also possess knowledge of the ten categories, such as the ability to maintain meditative stability as the deity, knowledge of the specific mudras of the tantra, and so forth,[7] and be skilled in drawing and visualizing the mandala in order to be able to lead the disciples into it during the initiation.

The master first performs a ground-breaking ceremony, then, before giving the initiation to the disciple, an extensive self-initiation.[8]

An initiation is an interaction between master and disciple, so in many ways the qualities of the vajra disciple are just as important as the qualities of the vajra master. If the disciple is not qualified, the empowerment will not take place. The qualities required of the disciple are stated in the *Vajra Garland Tantra* (*Vajramala Tantra*) as:

> Faithful and full of respect for the guru,
> Abiding always in the practice of virtue,
> With wrong view completely abandoned,
> Such a one must have received many teachings.
>
> Free of the faults of killing and harming,
> With his mind intent on liberating beings,
> Always diligent and very pure,
> These and others are the virtues he should have;
> But the best of all is strong faith.[9]

A disciple must come to his or her practice of tantra with conviction or faith, but that does not mean blind faith. True faith comes from an understanding of the Sutrayana practices, particularly from bodhichitta and the wisdom realizing emptiness.

We also need a strong conviction and unshakable faith in the vajra master and in the deity of the initiation, and for that we need good communication with the master and trust in him or her. To establish that trust, we need to understand the character and experience of the master giving the initiation. Lama Tsongkhapa in his *Fifty Verses* commentary says that we need to examine the master for up to twelve years before we reach a conclusion about whether he or she is the right master from whom to take initiation.

If all of these elements are in the place, we must still check if our motivation is correct. Are we taking the initiation because of bodhichitta? Can we really keep the commitments? Taking an initiation is a rare and precious opportunity. We need to approach it with the clearest motivation and greatest sincerity.

Guru Yoga

The teacher is as important as the deity to making Vajrayana practice effective. The guru-yoga section of a tantric sadhana involves actively seeing the vajra master as the enlightened being. In some texts by Indian masters, the guru-yoga section was combined with the section on deity yoga, but the Tibetan teachers have made it a separate practice. Most deity-yoga practices include at least a short practice of guru yoga at the beginning.

In deity yoga, after the preliminary prayers and before the main visualization and mantra recitation, there is usually a section where we make offerings to what is called the *merit field*. "Merit" refers to the positive imprints we make on our mental continuum from doing positive actions, and the "field" is the bases upon which we can generate merit through such things as offerings, prayers, and devotion. In tantric sadhanas, the merit field tends to be either a complex visualization of the deities, bodhisattvas, and lamas connected with the particular deity of our tantric practice or a simpler visualization of the guru. We can generate the greatest merit in connection with the vajra master, because that is the person we are closest to. But if we were to think of the vajra master as a normal person with delusions and faults, we would not collect much merit.

The essence of guru yoga is to see our clear-light mind—the subtlest level of our consciousness—as inseparable from the meditation deity and the guru who has given the initiation, the being we see as our root guru. Depending on the tantric practice, the guru-yoga section can be long and elaborate or very short, but it is always characterized by meditation on the inseparability of these three elements:

+ the clear-light mind of the practitioner
+ the practitioner's meditation deity
+ the practitioner's root guru

For instance, in the meditation manual we go through in chapter 4, visualizing the merit field involves visualizing His Holiness the Dalai Lama, the vajra master, as inseparable from the deity Avalokiteshvara situated at his heart, with a tiny seed syllable[10] at Avalokiteshvara's heart. This is often called the "three stacks" or the "three beings" (sattvas). This is not to say that there is a real Dalai Lama with a separate real Avalokiteshvara and a separate real seed syllable. All three beings are inseparably one. In the same way, during actual guru yoga, the guru, who is inseparable from the deity, enters into our heart and becomes inseparable from our own subtle mind. We then meditate on this inseparability.

The Initiation

The Sanskrit term for initiation is *abhisheka*, which is also often translated as "empowerment." It has many different connotations. There are three different kinds of initiations:

+ causal initiation
+ path initiation
+ resultant-state initiation

The first initiation, *causal initiation*, allows the practitioner to enter into Vajrayana and do a deity practice, thereby ripening his or her mind. The second initiation, *path initiation*, is given when the practitioner reaches an advanced stage and needs this kind of initiation to progress further. When the practitioner has fully purified all defilements and fully attained all qualities, the final initiation, the *resultant-state initiation*, is given. In this book, we will only deal with the causal initiation.

It is important to remember that the basis for taking any initiation is strong refuge, and not just the refuge of an individual liberation practitioner, but strong Mahayana refuge, where we determine to become enlightened as quickly as possible in order to help all living beings be free from suffering. We must also strive to cultivate not just aspiring bodhichitta, but engaged bodhichitta. The training of a bodhisattva on the universal liberation vehicle takes many lifetimes—eons even. For a Vajrayana practitioner the thought of waiting that long and of the suffering that all living beings must endure during that time is unbearable. In order to relieve their suffering as quickly possible, we determine to become enlightened without delay, no matter how hard the road is or how many difficulties need to be overcome. If we possess that special altruistic attitude and a deep understanding of emptiness, we have all the basic requirements for receiving the initiation, and so we can approach the vajra master to request a particular initiation into the deity that we are going to practice.

Although there are four classes of tantra, the middle two, charya and yoga, are not as common as kriya and highest yoga, especially in the Gelug tradition of Tibetan Buddhism. It is not obligatory that we start with the lowest tantra and work up to the highest, but it does help to receive a kriya tantra initiation first because of the relative simplicity of the practice. But whatever level we start from, we need to receive the initiation from a qualified vajra master.

THE PURPOSE OF AN INITIATION

A vajra master can perform two levels of initiation ceremonies. The first is called *wang* in Tibetan, which loosely means "belongs to me." This is what we generally think of as an initiation, a ceremony that gives someone the right to do this practice. But the term "initiation" can also be used to describe the Tibetan *jenang*. A *jenang* is also a ceremony that grants permission to practice a deity, but it is not considered an initiation because it does not have a vase initiation, which we discuss below. At the jenang the vajra master simply introduces the disciple to the deity through the blessing of the deity's body, speech, and mind. To receive jenang in a particular class of tantra, we need to have already received an initiation in either that class or in a higher one.

The main purpose of receiving an initiation—a *wang*—in a particular deity is to receive permission to practice that deity; visualize ourselves as that deity; use the hand implements of that deity such as the vajra and bell; study commentaries on the practice of that deity; and do the practices associated with that deity, usually in the form of a meditation practice from a sadhana.

There is also a reason to receive the initiation from a fully qualified vajra master in particular. Initiation given by a fully qualified master comes from his or her previous guru, who received it from his or her previous guru, and so on. In fact, the Tibetan word for tantra is *gyu*, which literally means "continuum" or "lineage." In this tradition what we receive has been handed down in a direct line from one realized practitioner to the next, all the way from the very first meditator who actualized the practice to the present day. We receive the initiation knowing that there is this continuity, and that the initiating master has actualized the practice with either a full mantra-recitation retreat or a direct vision of the deity. This absolute purity of the lineage of the practice is vital for the success of our own practice of the deity.

We are taking on the energy of this continuity of the practice when we receive an initiation. Without receiving an initiation, we can visualize the deity, recite the mantra, and read the texts, but our mind will not be in the position to do these things properly. It is fundamental to Vajrayana to have received permission to practice from a living being who is part of the lineage.

Receiving an initiation means more than just being present when one is given. It does not suffice to just sit there and receive the initiation substances; we have to follow the whole process of visualization. When His Holiness the Dalai Lama was asked at the end of a three-day Kalachakra initiation in Los Angeles in 1989 how many of the thousands of people present had actually received the initiation, he said, "Hardly anyone." And there were many respected lamas on the stage! Without our active participation, we cannot say that we have truly received the initiation.

Vajrayana requires not only strong participation but also great determination to actually practice the commitment we have taken on. We need to have first taken some precepts, such as one or more of the five lay vows.[11] Then we need to take the bodhisattva vows during the initiation. This is a requirement; if we are not ready to do this, we are not ready to receive the initiation. It is crucial to keep these vows as purely as we can. A prerequisite of receiving the bodhisattva vows is to have already received at least one set of individual liberation vows, such as the five lay vows or the monastic precepts. The Buddha himself said on many occasions that the Buddhist precepts are given gradually.

Thus initially we should take the lay vows, and then later take the monastic vows, and so forth.

THE PRELIMINARY STAGES OF AN INITIATION

During the initiation, you will be asked to meditate. The ritual is conducted in esoteric language, so it is helpful to have a good understanding of the process before taking an initiation.

The initiation is performed in three stages:

+ blessing the ground
+ the preliminary initiation (preparation)
+ the main initiation

The first stage of an initiation, *blessing the ground*, is the sole responsibility of the vajra master. The place where the initiation will take place is blessed with strong prayers. If a sand mandala is built in connection with the initiation, the completed mandala is also blessed by the vajra master.

In the second stage, the *preliminary initiation*, the vajra master gives refuge and the bodhisattva vows and, if it is a highest yoga tantra initiation, the tantric vows. The master introduces the disciples to the mandala of the deity by describing it, and that description forms part of the visualization that the disciples are supposed to hold.

The mandala, or celestial palace of the deity, is a square building, beautifully ornate, built on a huge double, or four-spoked, vajra. Some are surrounded by a ring of funeral grounds, fire, and a fence made of vajras. Every mandala has four doors, one in each cardinal direction. Before the end of the preliminary initiation, the vajra master will lead the disciples in their visualization to the eastern door so the disciples can stand at the entrance to the deity's mandala.

Lower classes of tantra initiations are generally given in one day, but some, such as the Thousand-Armed Avalokiteshvara "great" initiation, take two days. More complex initiations span two days or more; the Kalachakra initiation, for example, takes three. In those cases, the first day is spent in preparation, where the ground is blessed and the preliminary initiation is given.

At the end of the day, the vajra master gives each disciple a red protection or blessing string. These strings are a cubit in length (approximately the distance from the fingertip to the elbow) and have three knots. The disciples are also given two different lengths of *kusha* grass, said to be the grass the Buddha used as a meditation seat when he sat under the bodhi tree to become enlightened. Kusha grass is symbolic of purification; it is used to gain clear concentration. It is placed under the bed, the short piece crosswise under the pillow and the long piece lengthwise under the mattress. Finally, the disciples are asked to try to remember the dreams they have just before daybreak to see whether they contain any auspicious or inauspicious elements.

THE MAIN INITIATION

Only after the first two stages are complete can the main initiation take place. The complexity of the main initiation varies according to each disciple's individual level of tantra.

There are four levels of a causal initiation:

+ vase initiation
+ secret initiation
+ wisdom initiation
+ word initiation

The base initiation for all tantras is the *vase initiation*, which is divided into six smaller initiations. More vase initiations are given for higher tantras and fewer for lower. Thus a kriya tantra initiation has two, charya tantra has five, and yoga tantra has all six. Highest yoga tantra has all six vase initiations and the three additional initiations. Table 1 lists the six initiations of the vase initiation.

TABLE 1. VASE INITIATIONS WITHIN THE FOUR LEVELS OF TANTRA

INITIATION	KRIYA	CHARYA	YOGA	HIGHEST YOGA
water initiation	•	•	•	•
crown initiation	•	•	•	•
ribbon initiation		•	•	•
vajra-and-bell initiation		•	•	•
name initiation		•	•	•
vajra-master initiation			•	•

With the first vase initiation, the water initiation, the disciples are outside the eastern door of the mandala. Before they enter they are given a flower to make as an offering to the deity.[12] After giving the disciples an explanation of what is happening, the vajra master opens the eastern door and gives refuge and the bodhisattva vows again (and, if it is a highest yoga tantra initiation, the tantric vows). The vows are the same as the previous day's, but this time they are given inside the mandala rather than outside.

The water initiation is so called because the vajra master blesses water in a *bumpa* vase and passes it around for the disciples to sip in order to purify the five aggregates.[13] Through purification they are then able to visualize the deity.

The second initiation (and the last in kriya tantra) is the crown initiation. In the place where the initiation is taking place there will be a representation of a five-sectioned crown on the altar. This signifies the five Dhyani Buddhas, with each Dhyani Buddha associated with one particular aggregate.[14] Our ordinary appearance is of a body and mind with the five contaminated aggregates. In the resultant state of a Vajrayana practice, these turn into the five purified Dhyani Buddhas.

Sutrayana asserts that our aggregates are contaminated until we attain full enlightenment. In Vajrayana, there are various levels of subtlety of each aggregate, from gross and very contaminated to subtle and very subtly contaminated. But Vajrayana also asserts that there is basic purity to the aggregates at the subtlest level. They become purified through practice to become the five Dhyani Buddhas. Here, the crown of the crown initiation represents the purified state of the five aggregates, as the Dhyani Buddhas. Through this, the disciples visualize themselves—their five aggregates—as the deity.

Kriya tantra only has two of the five initiations within the vase initiation; both are meant to purify the body. If we do an initiation in the second class of tantra, charya, in addition to the water and crown initiations, we are also given the ribbon, vajra-and-bell, and name initiations. The ribbon initiation purifies the speech, the vajra-and-bell initiation purifies the mind, and the name initiation purifies the activities.

They are all called *vase initiations* because at the end of each initiation, the disciples are given a sip of water from the blessed vase. These five initiations are often referred to collectively as the *vajra disciple's initiations*.

In the third class of tantra, yoga tantra, the disciple receives the first five vase initiations and the vajra-master initiation. The vajra-master initiation is itself divided into four initiations:

+ prophecy
+ holding the vajra behavior
+ activities
+ introduction

In the *prophecy* initiation, the vajra master calls the disciple up (or a group representative if there is a big crowd) and asks him or her to throw a stick above a mandala that is divided into five sections—the four cardinal directions and the center. Where the stick falls determines the buddha family that the disciple belongs to. That is the prophecy. For instance, if the stick falls in the north, the vajra master will say, "In the future you will attain enlightenment in the aspect of Amoghasiddhi."

The next vajra-master initiation is the *holding the vajra behavior* initiation. After this initiation is given, the disciples are not allowed to reveal the secret deity to others. Because of the very subtle nature of tantric practice and our relationship with the meditation deity, there is great scope for misunderstanding and misuse if tantric instructions are heard out of context. For that reason, we are asked to keep our deity secret from everyone but our vajra brothers and sisters, those who have taken the same initiation that we have.

The third initiation is the *activities* initiation; it is similar to the vajra-and-bell initiation in charya tantra. In this initiation, the disciples are given a physical vajra and bell to hold, which symbolize method and wisdom. From that moment on, the disciples are not to be separate from the vajra and bell.

In the last vajra-master initiation, the *introduction* initiation, the vajra master introduces the disciples to the deity, who thus becomes their personal deity. After receiving the vajra-master initiation, taking the tantric vows, and finishing a retreat with that deity, the disciples are allowed to give these initiations to others.

There are three remaining initiations—the *secret*, *wisdom*, and *word initiations*—that are only given in highest yoga tantra.

Unlike the vase and vajra master initiations, these three initiations don't have any subdivisions, and only in the secret initiation are there any substances to be distributed. During these initiations the disciple should mainly meditate while the vajra master explains the implications of the initiation.

In highest yoga tantra the first initiation, the vase initiation, is given to allow the disciple to do the generation stage; these remaining three initiations are given so the disciple can do the completion stage. We will discuss the generation and completion stages of highest yoga tantra in the last three chapters of this book.

THE MANDALA

With the initiation we are allowed to practice the deity, which includes visualizing the celestial palace, or mandala, of the deity. There are two main kinds of mandalas: the *outer mandala* and the *inner mandala*. There is also a third mandala, the *concentration mandala*, where disciples with very advanced concentration are able to visualize the mandala without the external base, but this is very rare.

With the outer mandala, the vajra master performs the initiation using a mandala printed on paper or cloth or created in sand. Sand mandalas are usually only used for very big initiations, such as the Kalachakra, and they are usually created by a specially trained team of monks or nuns. These outer mandalas serve as the base for the initiation. This constructed mandala is not the actual mandala; the actual mandala is what is visualized during the initiation. The purpose of the constructed mandala is to help the vajra master explain the features of the actual mandala to the disciples as the master goes through the rituals of the initiation.

In some monasteries, there is also a three-dimensional mandala that is a large construction built just as the meditator is supposed to visualize it—it has a double-vajra base, four doors, and all the ornaments, and often has cut-away walls so the deities inside are visible. But these three-dimensional mandalas are not used as bases for initiations; initiations are only given based on printed, drawn, or sand mandalas.

The outer mandala is usually installed in a mandala house, a small structure with curtained walls. During the preliminary stages of the initiation, the disciples wear a red strip of cloth on their foreheads to signify being blindfolded because they are not initiated and therefore not ready to see the mandala. At the point in the initiation where the vajra master gives them permission, the curtains of the mandala house are opened to reveal the mandala, and the "blindfolds" are removed.

Within the actual mandala to be visualized there may be a single deity or many deities, depending on the initiation. For example, one of the Guhyasamaja mandalas has thirty-two deities, and one of the Heruka mandalas has sixty-two.

Each aspect of the mandala is significant: the four doors represent the four mindfulnesses or the four noble truths, the eight pillars represent the noble eightfold path, and so forth. Thus the mandala is not to be imagined as concrete or bricks—it is built with the realizations of the meditator.

The *inner mandala* is where the practitioner's entire mind and body is visualized first becoming a mandala in the sense of the abode of the deities, and then having the resident deities abide there. Many sadhanas give instructions for this practice following the preliminary prayers. A common instruction might be:

> Your aggregates, elements, senses, and sense objects, as well as your limbs, are the mandala complete with the five buddhas and their consorts, male and female bodhisattvas, and the wrathful protectors.

Not all deity practices have an inner mandala stage.

Apart from the outer and inner mandala, some tantras also include a *body mandala*, which is a general term referring to the practice of correlating the elements of the mandala with the parts of the practitioner's own body. Different deity practices explain different ways of doing this, but generally speaking, the elements of the body and the five sense consciousnesses are all visualized into the deity.

Vows and Commitments

As we have seen, taking vows is an integral part of every initiation. It is important to distinguish between vows and commitments, since you are likely to be given both during an initiation.

Vows (Skt. *samvara*; Tib. *dompa*) are the bodhisattva and tantric vows that are given during the initiation by the vajra master. They are based on previous vows taken by the disciple, such as the lay refuge vows, and they are the same for every deity. Thus if we have already taken the bodhisattva and tantric vows within a Yamantaka initiation and we are now going to take a Guhyasamaja initiation, the vows will be exactly the same.

The bodhisattva vows are eighteen root and forty-six secondary vows and relate to training the mind in the six perfections. They are vows we take to not commit various "downfalls" such as praising ourselves, not sharing the Dharma with others, holding perverted views, and so forth.[15] Asanga's *Bodhisattva's Grounds* says that we should be highly familiar with the vows before we receive them. The tantric vows, on the other hand, must be received before we can research them, due to their very subtle nature and the chance of them being misinterpreted if read purely out of curiosity.

The term *commitment* (Skt. *samaya*; Tib. *damtsig*) refers specifically to the relationship we have with the vajra master and how we must never do anything that breaks that special bond. Each tantra requires taking a different set of commitments. For example, part of the commitment of kriya tantra practice is to refrain from eating what are called *black foods*, which are generally listed as meat, fish, garlic, onions, eggs, and radishes.[16] These are classed as "black" because they are believed to excite the winds, thus making clear visualizations more difficult. Within highest yoga tantra, however, meat and alcohol are used symbolically in some practices, such as in the *Guru Puja*.

Initiations often include mantra-recitation commitments; these vary depending on the vajra master. For example, one vajra master could commit the practitioners to reciting a mantra 100,000 times over a lifetime, while another could require a commitment of a retreat of 600,000 recitations within one year.

We should take the vows and commitments very seriously. Many students take an initiation full of enthusiasm, but when it comes to the daily practice or the long retreat, that enthusiasm wanes. Accepting the commitments of a tantric practice is vowing we will follow the instructions of our vajra master. To willfully go against his or her instructions is the most serious breach of the guru-disciple relationship possible.

An initiation is more than just a ceremony that marks the start of our relationship with the deity of that initiation. It forges a strong bond with the vajra master and moves our mind away from the mundane, blind acceptance that this world we see is all there is into a subtler and vaster world that introduces us to our own mind at its most profound.

3 THE LOWER TANTRAS

OF THE FOUR CLASSES of tantra—kriya, charya, yoga, and highest yoga—many of the initiations given in the West are highest yoga tantra, and so there can be a sense that this is the important class and the others are in some way inferior. This is a misunderstanding. Even for those of you who have taken a highest yoga tantra initiation, it is vital to understand the lower tantras. In a verse autobiography, Lama Tsongkhapa says:

> Seeing clearly that without understanding
> The methods of the three lower tantras,
> My decision that highest yoga tantra is best of all
> Would be no more than an unsupported assertion,
> I therefore enquired deeply into
> The three types of action tantra.[17]

Without a proper understanding and direct profound experience of the lower tantras, it is very difficult to assert with confidence that highest yoga tantra is truly the supreme tantric practice. Lamas often give initiations in highest yoga tantra and praise it as best, but if we have not tested it, it really is "no more than an unsupported assertion" for us. Without understanding all the aspects of the lower tantras, there will be big holes in our practice when we try to actualize our deity practice at a deep level. It is therefore important for anybody seriously interested in Vajrayana to understand and appreciate the lower tantras. In this and the next chapter, we will look at an overview of them and then go through a kriya tantra meditation manual.

The Differences among the Four Classes of Tantra

INTERNAL AND EXTERNAL ACTIVITIES

Every tantric practice is made up of a mixture of practices that we call *internal activities*, such as visualization of the deity, and other practices called *external activities*, such as saying prayers and making the correct hand gestures.

The first class of tantra, kriya tantra, gets its name from the strong emphasis it places on the external activities. The Sanskrit word *kriya* is etymologically related to the word *karma*, which literally means "action." Thus kriya tantra places great importance on the physical actions we do in our practice, such as maintaining the cleanliness of our body, our environment, and the food we eat. If we are doing a retreat with four sessions, the retreat space must be cleaned in the morning before the first session, and we are encouraged to ensure our body is also clean before each session. We are also not supposed to eat black foods—food and drink that contaminate the body by disturbing the subtle winds.

Kriya tantra also prescribes a lot of mudras. *Mudras* are very precise hand movements or positions. Each mudra has a specific significance, such as the various offering mudras that signify the substances offered. Mudras must be done, and they must be done perfectly. Each of these practices is meant to help the practitioner develop concentration through external activities.

The second class of tantra is charya tantra. The name *charya*, which literally means "performance," comes from the emphasis on rituals and recitation in this class. There are many other elements of a deity practice, but the focus here is on knowing how to set up and perform a variety of rituals.

The third class is called *yoga tantra*. *Yoga* means "union," but it is rarely translated in English-language Vajrayana texts. Yoga tantra places more emphasis on internal activities, such as visualizations of the deity and mandala, than the first two classes of tantra.

The last class is called *highest yoga tantra* (Skt. *anuttara yoga tantra*). Here the emphasis is on internal yoga or union with the deity, achieved through practices involving the manipulation of the wind energies within the body. Another unique feature of highest yoga tantra is the practice of taking death, intermediate state, and rebirth into the path. This is perhaps the biggest difference between the three lower classes of tantra and highest yoga tantra, since this is the key method to actualize the resultant stage—the union of the illusory body and the clear-light mind. When we can join the most subtle mind with the most subtle of the psychic winds that abides in the center of the central channel, this is the union of the illusory body and the clear-light mind; this is enlightenment itself.

There is no hard-and-fast rule that we must start with a kriya tantra practice and then graduate to a higher one, but it is worthwhile to do so. This is because of the relative simplicity of kriya tantra practice. In addition, with kriya tantra we only take bodhisattva vows, whereas with highest yoga tantra we take both bodhisattva vows and tantric vows. It is advisable to have a fair amount of experience trying to keep the bodhisattva vows before progressing to the more profound and subtle tantric vows.

This progression is also helpful for deity visualizations. In kriya tantra, deities are usually peaceful and fairly simple to visualize, with one face and two or four arms, but in the higher tantra classes, deities often have many faces and arms and can be quite visually complex.

Subduing the Vital Wind

Both the lower and higher tantras have a practice called *subduing the vital wind*, which is also commonly known by its Sanskrit name, *pranayama* (Tib. *tsogsol*). Although both lower tantra and higher tantra pranayama involve manipulating the body's wind energies by working with the breath, they are not the same practice.

Various winds (Skt. *vayu*) circulate in the body—the upward-moving wind, the downward-voiding wind, and so forth—and keep the body functioning. *Prana*, the vital wind, or life-supporting wind, is one of those basic winds. *Pranayama* in kriya tantra means trying to stop conceptual thought by holding the breath with a technique called *vase breathing*. This is a very profound and powerful technique, especially when combined with the visualization of our mind as a moon disc at our heart.

In normal life, these wind energies are the force that allows our various consciousnesses to arise: our eye consciousness to see color and form, our ear consciousness to hear sounds, our mental consciousness to remember the past and dream of the future, and so forth. We are all experiencing sensory and mental events continuously without consciously considering how these sense consciousnesses function. But of course there must be some energy within us that allows all of this to happen. In order to see shapes and color, we need more than an eye and an object of consciousness; we need something that carries the consciousness and allows it to make the connection. The analogy that is often given in Vajrayana teachings is of a blind person and a crippled person. There is nothing wrong with the blind person's legs, but he can't walk because he has no way of seeing where he is going. The crippled person can't walk at all, but he has sight. When the two meet, the crippled person can sit on the blind person's shoulders and direct him, and they can both get where they want to go. It is said the consciousnesses and wind energy perform together in the same way. We use these winds in vase breathing.

The way to subdue our vital wind in kriya tantra is basically to hold the breath—our natural breathing—for as long as possible. The first step is cleansing the channels, a practice often called *nine-point breathing*. For this practice, we need a good understanding of what the channels and chakras are. We will discuss this in more detail in chapter 7, but a brief description will be helpful here.

The winds run along myriad tiny channels that fill our body running roughly parallel with the physical nervous system. Among those there are three main ones: the central channel and the two associated channels that run on either side of it, starting at the center of the eyebrows for the central channel and the nostrils for the side channels. Each of the nine parts of the nine-point breathing involves bringing the wind down one channel and up the other, cleansing it. So with the first three breaths we breathe in the right nostril, imagining the winds in the form of bright white light passing down the right channel and across to the left one, where, with the exhalation, the wind purifies it, visualized as black smoke or oily black sludge passing out of the left nostril and dispersing into space. For the next three rounds, the right channel is cleansed in this way, and then for the last three rounds the winds pass down both side channels and into the central one, cleansing that.

After that we can engage in the practice of vase breathing, where the prana is held between the navel and heart by a combination of holding the breath and tensing the pelvic muscles, creating a tension that traps the wind energy in that area. Done correctly, this practice effectively stops conceptual thought and distractions and allows strong and vivid visualizations. The practice of vase breathing is presented in more detail at the end of the next chapter.

The practice of pranayama in highest yoga tantra involves moving our subtle winds into the central channel and loosening the knots around our heart chakra so that the winds can eventually be dissolved into the indestructible drop in our heart, as we will see in chapter 8. The two pranayamas also differ with regard to when in the practitioner's development they are done. The practice of pranayama in the lower tantras can be done with an intellectual understanding of emptiness. Highest yoga tantra pranayama, however, requires a realization of emptiness.

The purpose of the two practices is also different. In the lower tantras the purpose of pranayama is to increase concentration, have a clear visualization of the deity, and even to prolong life. In highest yoga tantra the purpose is to unblock the central channel so the winds can dissolve in our heart, allowing us to realize buddhahood. This completion-stage practice is the most profound practice we can do.

Yoga with Sign

Highest yoga tantra is divided into generation-stage practices and completion-stage practices. The lower three schools do not have these stages. Instead, they are divided into two stages that are known as *yoga with sign* and *yoga without sign*.

"Sign" means to have a sense of ourselves as truly existing. When we meditate on the deity, because we only have a conceptual understanding of emptiness, all the aspects of the practice are still seen as existing intrinsically. This is yoga with sign. Yoga without sign is thus the practice where that grasping at true existence has been overcome.

Yoga with sign is the starting point of all lower-tantra visualizations. These deity-yoga visualization practices offer a unique way of cultivating a very sharp and deep concentration. Thus the three branches of yoga with sign are called the *three concentrations*. They are:

* the concentration of the four branches of recitation
* the concentration of abiding in fire
* the concentration of abiding in sound

THE CONCENTRATION OF THE FOUR BRANCHES OF RECITATION

Most of the elements of a deity practice based on a sadhana are included in the concentration of the four branches of recitation. If you already have a commitment of a kriya tantra or charya tantra deity practice and use a sadhana, you will probably be going through these stages. The sadhana may not categorize them in this way, but it is very helpful to understand these four divisions to see how this process leads us to an ever more subtle and profound level of concentration. The four branches that give this concentration its name are:

* abiding on the basis of another
* abiding on the basis of oneself
* abiding on the basis of mind
* abiding on the basis of sound

The first branch is *abiding on the basis of another*. "Another" refers to the deity that we have visualized in front of us, also called the *front-generation deity*. This sets us up for part of the practice later on where we visualize the mantra in the deity's heart and then recite the mantra. At that time, we are basing our visualization on the "other," as opposed to the self-generation. In the sadhana we look at in the next chapter, *The Inseparability of the Guru and Avalokiteshvara*, this comes in the section called "visualizing the merit field."

The second branch, *abiding on the basis of oneself*, happens when we visualize ourselves as the deity through self-generation. In *Inseparability*, this branch and the other two branches below come in the section called "merging of the spiritual master."

In many kriya tantra practices, generating ourselves as the deity is not there, or it is not explicit. Some traditions also say that we should not generate ourselves as the deity unless we have had a "great" kriya tantra initiation—such as the two-day great Avalokiteshvara—or a highest yoga tantra initiation. It is good to check with your teacher about this before you take on this aspect of the practice. What we will look at below is a kriya tantra practice that involves generating ourselves as a deity.

In the lower tantras, self-generation involves six stages, which are called the *six deities*. Some manuals list these explicitly (the section of the *nyungné* practice included as appendix 2 does this), but many simply explain the steps. Many don't even do that, so it is good to understand the process that is done each time. The six deities are:

+ the deity of emptiness
+ the deity of sound
+ the deity of letter
+ the deity of form
+ the deity of mudra
+ the deity of symbol

The first step, the *deity of emptiness* or the *ultimate deity*, is a meditation on emptiness. This is the base upon which we do the remaining five steps. This step is the substantial cause for us to see ourselves as a deity and hold that divine identity. As we have seen, visualizing our ordinary body as a deity's body or our ordinary consciousness as a divine consciousness is completely mistaken. Instead, at this stage in the practice we need to reinforce and enhance whatever understanding of emptiness we have. Some sadhanas give some explanation of emptiness to help arouse that understanding; others just instruct the practitioner to do the meditation. We try to bring a strong sense of the emptiness of ourselves and what we visualize, at least understanding that this is so, even though we might not at this stage have a realization of this. With that, we can move to the next stage, the deity of sound.

With the *deity of sound*, the sound of the mantra—*Om mani padme hum* in the case of *Inseparability*—spontaneously arises from the sphere of emptiness. It is not that we are speaking the mantra in our head. Rather the sound is just there, and it fills the entire space—it "pervades the realms of space"—like an echo in a great hall. We feel the entire environment become filled with the sound of this mantra.

The third step in building up the visualization is the *deity of letter*. The sound becomes visible in the form of the letters of the mantra. Our mind and the deity are inseparable in suchness—that is, in the nature of being empty of any intrinsic nature—even while they simultaneously manifest as the different shapes of the letters of the mantra.

At this stage we have not yet visualized the complete deity, but our mind, holding the undifferentiated suchness of ourselves and the deity, becomes a moon disc at our heart, a flat circle of bright white light. Then the sound of the mantra, which is resonating throughout the whole of space, descends to the middle of the moon disc and gradually transforms into the syllables of the mantra. The syllables differ for each deity—for Avalokiteshvara it would be the six white syllables; for Vajrasattva it would be either the full hundred-syllable Vajrasattva mantra or simply *Om vajrasattva*, both white; and so forth. The syllables are not flat on the moon disc; they stand upright, facing inward, and are usually oriented clockwise.

Some people feel that the syllables should face outward, because then we—that is, the meditator sitting on a meditation cushion looking at all this—can see them. Otherwise, their backs are turned to us as if they dislike us. But we should not see ourselves as outside this visualization. The manual says our mind is the moon disc, and that is where our mind should be. Then we are in the middle, surrounded by the mantra garland. Suddenly this whole visualization seems a lot more difficult, I suspect!

It is important to recognize that there is a process happening here. From emptiness (the deity of emptiness), the sound of the mantra (the deity of sound) arises. Then we visualize the nature of our mind, the mind that realizes emptiness. That mind transforms into a moon disc, and the mantra slowly transforms from sound to syllables standing on the moon disc.

With the *deity of form*, we visualize the complete deity. For example, if we are following *Inseparability*, the moon disc with Avalokiteshvara's mantra is there at our heart, and there arises Avalokiteshvara with one face and four arms. This is the deity of form. The sadhana in appendix 2 describes the deity of the *nyungné* practice, Thousand-Armed Avalokiteshvara, in detail. Likewise, in every sadhana there will be a detailed description of the deity at this stage—the form, the clothes, the hand gestures, the implements, and so forth—and that is what we should try our best to visualize.

After we have generated ourselves as the full deity, the fifth step is the *deity of mudra*. At our forehead, we visualize a white syllable *om*; at our throat, a red syllable *ah*; and at our heart, a blue syllable *hum*:

At the top of the *hum* is a circle. Within this circle we visualize a moon disc, and on the middle of that moon disc, standing upright, we visualize the syllable for the deity we are using. For Avalokiteshvara, use *hrih*:

In kriya tantra there are three lineages of deities, and the Avalokiteshvara practice belongs to the lotus or *padma* lineage. During this step of the practice we do the lotus mudra, where thumb and ring fingers touch, the little fingers of each hand cross each other, and the rest of the fingers stretch straight out, forming the shape of a lotus. The actual mudra is to place our hands in this position and then touch our forehead, throat, heart, right shoulder, and finally left shoulder. That is the *deity of mudra.*

In the final step, the *deity of symbol* or the *deity of sign*, we are no longer in the process of becoming the deity but rather strongly feel we *are* that deity. Through the preceding practices—the sound, the mantra syllables, the actual form of the deity, the three syllables, and finally the *hrih* in the circle of the *hum*—our concentration has grown finer, sharper, and more vivid. Now it is incredibly strong and stable.

Now, from the letter *hrih* at our heart as a deity, streams of nectar radiate in all directions, eliminating all the suffering and obstacles afflicting every sentient being. Then those same streams invoke billions and billions of deities, and these are then absorbed back into our heart, bringing us the blessings and understandings of all the buddhas and bodhisattvas. Ling Rinpoche, a tutor of His Holiness the Dalai Lama, once explained we should imagine ourselves on a mountain, watching in the far distance as rain falls in every direction, so heavily that the individual drops seem to be just one mass of rain. In the same way, the multitudes of deities come closer and closer and melt into each other, becoming a single deity. We can visualize this composite deity in any size that suits us. In *Inseparability*, it is Avalokiteshvara, in oneness with His Holiness the Dalai Lama, who dissolves into us, merging with our body like a bubble that hits it, bursts, and is absorbed. Radiant light then shines forth, purifying all defects in all beings and all impure appearances.

Quite often at this stage of the visualization, we say the mantra *Jah hum bam hoh.* As we say this, four things happen. When we say *jah*, the single deity comes above our head; when we say *hum* it dissolves into us; with *bam* we become inseparable from the deity; and with *hoh* we cultivate great joy. Having received the blessings of all the buddhas and bodhisattvas and merged our identity with the spiritual master in the form of the deity, we now feel strongly that we ourselves are truly that deity.

Thus far we have visualized the deity in front and then visualized ourselves as the deity using these six steps or "deities." The third branch, *abiding on the basis of mind*, takes the visualization one step further. The "mind" that is the basis of this stage is our own mind visualized in the form of a moon disc: a flat disc of brilliant white light at our heart chakra. We visualize the mantra in Sanskrit on top of the moon disc and then recite the mantra.

The final branch is *abiding on the basis of sound*. Here we imagine the mantra at our own heart or at the heart of the deity in front of us, this time not as syllables or letters but as the actual "sound" of the mantra. We then recite the mantra again. These stages are all practiced in conjunction with the practice of pranayama and increasing our concentration through vase breathing.

All four branches of the practice refer to different ways of reciting the mantra. The mantra may take different forms—syllables at the deity's heart, syllables at our own heart, sound moving backward and forward, and so forth—but its purpose is always to help develop a strong, sharp concentration.

THE CONCENTRATIONS OF ABIDING IN FIRE AND ABIDING IN SOUND

The second stage of yoga with sign is the *concentration of abiding in fire*. By now we will have become quite proficient in holding the visualization of the deity in front of us, of ourselves as the deity, of our mind as a moon disc at our heart, and of the mantra garland on that moon disc. At this stage we take our concentration to an even more profound level.

By this stage, through verbal and mental mantra recitation, we have reached a level of concentration that is verging on real calm abiding (Skt. *shamatha*). Every part of the process, from the refuge prayers onward, has honed and deepened this concentration, making it subtler and more profound.

Again, I will take the example of the Avalokiteshvara practice in *Inseparability*. We have done the last of the six deities of the concentration on abiding in the four recitations, the mental mantra recitation or deity of symbol. We see ourselves as Avalokiteshvara with an identical Avalokiteshvara in front of us. Now, in order to increase the concentration, we do the meditation with front-generation (abiding in others) and self-generation (abiding in self). Bringing all the elements of the visualization into clear focus, we cultivate the thought that they are empty of inherent existence. Moving from the grosser elements of the deity's appearance—hands, implements, clothing, and so forth—to the more subtle elements of the visualization—the deity's sense consciousnesses—we finally contemplate the emptiness of even the mental consciousness of the deity. We think that everything is empty of inherent existence.

When we reach the subtlest level of understanding of emptiness that we can, we hold our breath in the practice of vase breathing we looked at above. When we reach the subtlest mind we are capable of realizing, and we can no longer hold the breath, we exhale. Now we visualize ourselves as the deity, with a flat moon disc at our heart that is in the nature of our own mind. This is the same visualization we have already done during the four branches of recitation, but now on the moon disc there is a small flame, like that from a bright thin candle. The bottom is slightly thicker than the top, as real flames are, but it is not moving. In the middle of that flame is our own mind that had earlier realized emptiness.

So again there is a process of becoming more and more subtle. We meditate on ourselves as the deity, first the entire deity and then focusing on the various aspects of the deity. Then we meditate on our five sense consciousnesses and their emptiness, and then we move to the mind, at which stage we hold our breathing. When we can no longer hold the breath, we exhale; we repeat the process when ready. This is repeated many times.

In the next stage of the meditation, in the middle of the flame is the sound of the mantra—in Avalokiteshvara's case, *Om mani padme hum*. Unlike the sound of the mantra we meditated on previously, here the mantra is like the resonance of a bell that has stopped ringing. Think of when a bell is rung and then set down on a table; it is like the residue of the sound rather than the sound itself. Our entire mind is focused on that sound in the middle of the flame. The aspect of the sound of the mantra is in the nature of our own mind with ourselves as the deity realizing emptiness. When we can hold the breath no longer, we gradually exhale, focusing our mind on the deity as we do so.

We repeat this step many times, with the moon disc at our heart in the nature of our mind, the very bright small flame on the moon disc, and within that flame the nature of our mind realizing emptiness and the sound of the mantra.

This meditation is said to bring a practitioner's mind to full calm abiding. The previous meditations, such as the six steps of building up the self-generation, will help, but alone they are not powerful enough. This meditation is a special feature of the lower tantras. We can achieve calm abiding through highest yoga tantra, or through Sutrayana, or even through non-Buddhist philosophies, but the methods are different. Lower tantra gives us an extremely quick and skillful way of achieving this penetrating state.

In addition to giving rise to the state of calm abiding, this meditation can have other incredible effects. Successful practitioners of the concentration of abiding in fire are said to lose their dependence on the food and drink they once needed for survival.

When concentration is cultivated in this particular fashion in lower tantra, a feeling of tremendous bliss is felt alongside great mental and physical pliancy. This feeling is so intense that some practitioners are said to mistake it for liberation. (As someone with absolutely no concentration myself, I think I would quite like to risk making that mistake!) This phenomenon occurs because the concentration is so great that even subtle mental disturbances temporarily cease. Unfortunately the practice does not lead to the permanent cessation of our three poisonous minds.[18]

Furthermore, holding the breathing with this meditation on the flame at the heart on the moon disc increases the heat in the body, inducing a sense of physical and mental bliss. You may be familiar with the practice of *tumo*, or "inner heat" meditation, in highest yoga tantra. Although there are some similarities between the two practices, what we are describing here is something different.

The third and final concentration of yoga with sign is *the concentration of abiding in sound*. Similarly to the concentration of abiding in fire, here again we meditate on ourselves as the deity and move from the grosser aspects of visualization to the more subtle, seeing them all as empty of inherent existence. When we reach that strong understanding of emptiness of the subtlest aspect of the visualization, we hold our breath, and when we release our breath, we visualize ourselves as the deity with the moon disc in the nature of our own mind with a bright flame at its center.

This is where the visualization of abiding in sound becomes more subtle: here on the moon disc at our heart as the self-generation deity is another deity. It is in the same form as the self-generation, such as Avalokiteshvara or Tara, but very tiny. At that deity's heart is a tiny, bright flame, and in that flame, as in the previous concentration, is our own mind realizing emptiness, which manifests into the sound of the mantra. In the previous concentration, our mind focused on the flame; here we focus only on the sound that is inside the flame.

When we can no longer hold our breath, we gently release the breath and focus on ourselves as the deity or the front-generation deity. When we are ready, we repeat the process.

It is said that when a practitioner is successful in abiding in sound, he or she will naturally and spontaneously hear the entire mantra without sequence. Think of the way we normally hear *Om mani padme hum*—the *om* precedes the *mani* that precedes the *padme* that precedes the *hum*. The successful practitioner hears all six syllables of the mantra at once, simultaneously and without distinction. This is the concentration of abiding in sound.

Yoga without Sign

As we have seen, the lower tantras are divided into yoga with sign, where we have not realized emptiness, and yoga without sign, where we have. In order to progress through the stages of yoga with sign, we need a very good understanding of emptiness—any tantric practice rests on that—but there is still a conceptual consciousness there.

By this stage we have already attained full calm abiding from our yoga with sign practice, and we have a very deep understanding of emptiness. Now the main purpose of the meditation is to fully develop special insight (Skt. *vipashyana*) and realize emptiness within the deity practice. Unlike yoga with sign, where there are stages leading to the union of calm abiding with special insight, here our whole focus is that union.

At this stage we can clearly and easily hold ourselves as the deity as well as the entire environment of the deity, the moon disc, the mantra garland, and so forth. Our entire practice is suffused with a strong sense that we ourselves, and the objects of our meditation, are all completely empty of inherent existence.

With the basis of these two aspects—the clear appearance of the deity and environment, and the emptiness of the objects of meditation—we can slowly start to engage in analytical meditation. First we analyze the mandala and the actual deity element by element in order to fully determine whether there is a scrap of inherent existence within a single atom of them.

Holding a clear appearance and doing an analytical meditation at the same time is extremely difficult. At first the appearance will waver. Whenever that happens we return to the calm abiding and hold the clear appearance until it has stabilized again. Then we slowly begin to renew the sense of their lack of inherent existence. When those two elements are strong again, we can resume the analytical meditation. In that way calm abiding and insight meditation are slowly integrated. When we can do these two meditations simultaneously, it is called the *union of calm abiding and special insight,* the union of shamatha and vipashyana.

The next stage is to do this again and again, deepening the experience until finally that profound understanding of emptiness becomes a direct realization. This is analogous to attaining the path of seeing in Sutrayana. Once we have a direct realization of emptiness, the root of cyclic existence can easily be eliminated, and liberation will be attained.

Earlier meditations involved abiding in sound. This meditation is called *bestowing liberation at the end of sound* because we have now gone beyond that to a direct realization of emptiness and liberation. The nonconceptual realization of emptiness that marks this stage is what makes this yoga without sign.

4 PRACTICING KRIYA TANTRA

A Kriya Tantra Sadhana

IN THIS CHAPTER, we will use a sadhana to work through a kriya tantra practice to see clearly what it entails. Although here we are focusing on kriya tantra, if we can understand this meditation manual well, we can also easily apply that knowledge to charya tantra practice. The sadhana we will be using is *The Inseparability of the Guru and Avalokiteshvara*, hereafter referred to as *Inseparability*. It was composed by His Holiness the Dalai Lama when he was quite young. The full text is reproduced in appendix 1.[19]

Perhaps you are new to Vajrayana and this is the first time you have read anything about how a deity practice works. Or perhaps you already have a commitment to do a daily meditation session based on a sadhana of a particular deity but have never received instructions on the structure of the manual. Either way, I hope this chapter will show you how to use these manuals to take your meditation deeper, giving you the opportunity to develop richer realizations.

These manuals are designed to profoundly change your mindset from the ordinary to the extraordinary. The language and the visualizations used may seem exotic, but the psychology behind them is flawless. They lead you from self-involvement and confusion to a deep, selfless wisdom; to actual bodhichitta and a wisdom realizing emptiness.

Before you start a session with a sadhana, cultivate the thought that this is the right and proper way to meditate on that particular deity. Hopefully, through what you have read and studied about Vajrayana, you will already see that a tantric sadhana is an incredibly powerful and skillful tool in transforming the mind. Such a belief is very beneficial, as it adds conviction to your practice.

Your initial motivation must be to do whatever is necessary to develop a fully awakened mind as soon as possible in order to benefit all living beings—that is, bodhichitta. Any lesser motivation is insufficient for a practice as powerful as Vajrayana.

Once you have developed that foundation, you may sit on the meditation cushion, and making sure that your mind is clear and you have the right attitude, you can begin the practice.

Offerings

The second "limb" of the seven-limb prayer in the section called *accumulating merit* is making offerings, and many sadhanas have a discrete section where extensive offerings are made. You should have already laid out your offerings on the altar before the actual session, either simple water bowls or representations of the various substances. The offerings are:

Sanskrit	English
argham	water (for washing)
padyam	water (for drinking)
pushpe	flowers
dhupe	incense
aloke	light
gandhe	perfume
naivedya	food
shabda	music

The way Tibetans pronounce these Sanskrit words is slightly different but is more commonly heard. They are, respectively: *argum, pardyum, pupay, dupay, alokay, genday, nyuday,* and *shabda.*

The two waters are not actually counted as offerings; the first water is for washing feet, and the second is for drinking. The actual offerings are flowers, incense, light, perfume, food, and music. Each offering is a gift of pleasure to one of the six senses. They correspond to the things a host in India would traditionally offer a beloved guest—first water to clean the feet, then water to drink, then flowers to delight the eyes, incense to delight the nose, and so forth.

It's important to remember that when you make these offerings in your practice, they are not ordinary flowers or incense. When they are visualized and offered with a strong sense of emptiness, and hopefully a strong bodhichitta motivation, they become incredibly potent. By making these beautiful offerings to yourself as the deity, you create a powerful seed for your own future buddhahood.

There are various mantras and mudras that are also an important part of making offerings. (These do not come into *Inseparability,* but it is good to introduce them as you will certainly use them if you do other kriya tantra practices.) As you make each offering, you also say a mantra that asks the deity to enjoy that particular offering. For example, the mantra for the first water offering of the Avalokiteshvara practice is *Om Avalokiteshvara saparivara argham praticcha hum svaha.* The template of the mantra is generally the same; only the name of the deity—here Avalokiteshvara—and the name of the offering—here *argham* or water—change. Thus the mantra for the second water offering would be *Om Avalokiteshvara saparivara padyam praticcha hum svaha,* and so forth.

Each offering also has an accompanying mudra, where the action of the hands represents the respective offering. Because kriya tantra emphasizes doing actions correctly and precisely, you should only learn mudras from somebody who knows them well. Not only do the mudras change depending on the class of tantra, but they also differ depending on the lineage. Thus mudras done within the Kagyu lineage will be subtly different from those done in the Gelug lineage and so forth.

THE SADHANA

In Vajrayana we practice a structured meditation that we take from a meditation manual, or *sadhana*. A meditation manual is just that: a manual that shows us how to do the meditations associated with a particular deity. There are three main parts of a meditation session using a sadhana:

+ the preliminary practices
+ the main deity practice
+ the dedication

Many sadhanas also include a guru yoga section after the preliminary practices. Within these practices there are prayers to recite, offerings to make, and meditations to do. Although there are differences in the various sadhanas of the various classes of tantra, they also have many common features. Therefore it is worthwhile for any practitioner to understand how sadhanas work.

As we have seen, the first stage of yoga with sign, the concentration of the four branches of recitation, is the starting point of all lower-tantra visualizations. But before you get to that stage, you need to complete the preliminary practices. This is a vital part of any meditation, one that cannot be overemphasized.

There are two distinct sets of practices within the preliminary practices: the initial prayers and establishing the environment. In *Inseparability*, there are three prayers followed by two stages of purification:

+ refuge prayer
+ prayer for generating bodhichitta

* the four immeasurable thoughts prayer
* purification of place
* purification of offerings

Guru yoga and accumulating merit are also part of the preliminary practices.

REFUGE AND PURIFICATION

After spending some time settling the mind with something like a meditation concentrating on the breath, feel that you are in the presence of the Buddha. If you have a statue of the Buddha or another deity in front of you, do not feel that the Buddha is present in the form of that statue but that he is present as an actual living being with all his great qualities. If you can, imagine that all the other great spiritual teachers are also present.

Because the motivation you start any action with determines how beneficial or harmful the result of that action will be, it is always best to begin anything with as vast a motivation as possible. Therefore, the right motivation at the beginning of the practice is crucial. This is why taking refuge and generating the mind of bodhichitta commences any tantric practice.

In the presence of the Buddha and all the other spiritual teachers, strongly cultivate the thought that you are going to take refuge in the Three Jewels in order to free yourself and all living beings from cyclic existence. Then recite the refuge prayer, three times, and then the prayer for generating bodhichitta. This hugely powerful aspiration—wanting to benefit all living beings without exception and without discrimination—is motivated by great compassion. With that compassion, aspire to give help of all different kinds to all living beings—from their basic needs of food, shelter, and medicine, all the way up to the happiness of enlightenment.

The last prayer is the prayer of the four immeasurable thoughts, to develop the four great minds of love, compassion, joy, and equanimity. There is a long version of this prayer, with three or four lines for each immeasurable thought, but the short version used in *Inseparability* is also common. With either prayer, spend some time in meditation after each thought to contemplate its meaning.

THE PURIFICATION OF THE PLACE

After the preparatory prayers, the actual practice begins with the purification of the place and the purification of the offerings. With purification, you replace the sense of the ordinariness of the location of your meditation with a sense of it being some special, divine environment. For example, the prayers invoke the image of the surface of the earth being like lapis lazuli.[20] As you read the first prayer, imagine as strongly as possible that the place and the things around you are free from faults and impurities; imagine it as a pure environment.

The next step is to purify the offerings in the same way. Perhaps you have a set of water bowls on your altar, or perhaps you just visualize them. In either case it is important that you don't see these as ordinary either. These water bowls, or whatever actual substances you use as a base, become purified when you no longer see them as ordinary but as divine. This is also, of course, a purification of your mind. Through the power of your visualization, you can turn the water bowls into universes filled with every kind of divine substance, truly wonderful offerings to the buddhas of the merit field. There is also a mantra that increases the power of the offerings.

VISUALIZING THE MERIT FIELD

After the purification of the offerings come the visualizations. The first is the visualization of the merit field. In many sadhanas this is a visualization of the guru, the vajra master who gave them the initiation, who is considered the supreme merit field. In *Inseparability*, the merit field visualized is His Holiness the Dalai Lama.

Before you do the visualization, briefly meditate on emptiness. Ideally you begin with some analytical meditation on emptiness, and when your mind clearly realizes emptiness, you then do a single-pointed meditation for stability. A simpler practice is to clearly and strongly think that things and events, including yourself as a meditator and the activities that you are doing, are all entirely without intrinsic nature. Then, from within that understanding of emptiness, you visualize the vajra master in front of you.

Then, one and a half meters in front of you at the same height as your forehead, visualize a beautiful throne, vast and expansive. Entirely covering the throne is a lotus, and on that there is a sun disc and a moon disc.[21] On the moon disc is the guru (in this case, His Holiness) wearing the robes of a fully ordained monk. His right hand is at his heart in the gesture of expounding Dharma; his left hand is resting in his lap in the meditation mudra holding a thousand-spoked wheel.

Strongly think that His Holiness the Dalai Lama is the embodiment of Avalokiteshvara. Since Avalokiteshvara is the Compassion Buddha, here we are envisioning His Holiness as the embodiment of all the buddhas' compassion.

His Holiness' forehead is marked with a white letter *om*, at his throat is the red letter *ah*, and at his heart is the blue letter *hum*. Within His Holiness' heart, Four-Armed Avalokiteshvara sits on a lotus and moon disc. Avalokiteshvara's upper two hands are placed together at his heart holding a jewel. His lower two hands hold a crystal rosary and a white lotus that supports a book and a sword,[22] and at his heart is a white letter *hrih*. These details are described at length in *Inseparability*.

This visualization has three important levels: His Holiness the Dalai Lama, the Avalokiteshvara at his heart, and the letter *hrih* at

Avalokiteshvara's heart. These are called the *three stacked beings*, or *sattvas*: the commitment being (Skt. *samayasattva*), the wisdom being (*jñanasattva*), and the concentration being (*samadhisattva*).

This sort of highly detailed visualization is difficult for many people. I recommend two ways of developing your skills. One technique is to start with an outline of the shape of the deity, sort of like a blueprint. When you can hold that image clearly, you can slowly start to fill in the details, adding the face, body, clothes, and so forth, bit by bit. The other option is to concentrate on one part of the visualization, such as the forehead or the arms. Again, once you can hold that image clearly, you can then begin to build the whole deity.

The goal is to hold this initial visualization of the merit field—that is, the guru—for the whole session, but as you will see, things get more complicated. You can leave it in the background so that it is always there but not focused on specifically, like when a camera focuses on something in the foreground and the background remains blurry. Alternatively, you can dissolve the merit field into emptiness at the end of this part of the session.

The Seven-Limb Prayer and Mandala Offering

Having created this initial visualization, you then say the seven-limb prayer and make a mandala offering. The "seven limbs" of the prayer are prostrating, offering, confessing, rejoicing, requesting the guru deity to turn the wheel of Dharma, entreating him or her to remain, and dedicating the merits created. Engaging in these seven different practices makes the mind susceptible to the practice. For example, the purpose of offering prostrations—in this case, to the merit field, to your own guru—is to reduce and eventually eliminate negative pride and behavior. This is "accumulating merit" in the sense of freeing your mind from obstacles and ripening it so it can easily and effectively do these practices. After completing these seven practices, you give either a short or long mandala offering.

There are short and long versions of the mandala offering prayer, which is a visualization and prayer where you imagine the entire world system and all precious objects offered to the merit field of all the buddhas and bodhisattvas. This is a very common practice in Tibetan Buddhism. Here, because you are making this incredible offering to the being you have the strongest connection with, your guru, the merit you generate is huge.

The Main Deity Practice

In many sadhanas the biggest part of the preliminary practices is accumulating merit. In *Inseparability*, however, the focus is on guru yoga.

The first part of this is called "blessing by the master" in the sadhana. Now, from the *hrih* in the heart of the Avalokiteshvara at the heart of His Holiness the Dalai Lama, rays of five colors, representing the five primordial wisdoms, flow into you, eliminating all your obscurations and endowing you with all spiritual attainments. As this happens, you recite His Holiness' name mantra as many times as possible.

After that, there is a long lamrim prayer, where you ask the guru to bestow on you the various realizations of the stages of the path.

Then comes the section called "merging of the spiritual master." The guru—in this case, His Holiness the Dalai Lama, Avalokiteshvara, and the letter *hrih*, the threefold stack that until this point has been visualized in front of you—now dissolves into you through your crown and descends to your heart, where it dissolves into the indestructible drop at the center of your heart chakra. You then meditate that your subtlest mind, which is the clear-light mind, becomes inseparable from the guru and the deity at his heart.

With yourself as the deity, you refine your concentration using the three branches of the yoga with sign we looked at in the previous chapter. At first, the visualization is rough and inexact, but as you slowly work through the four branches of recitation, generating yourself as the deity using the six stages, or "deities," your meditation develops, becoming more focused and vivid. Finally, you are able to move to the last two concentrations of abiding in fire and abiding in sound. I suspect it will take a long time for any of us to reach that level.

At this point in the sadhana, you recite the mantra. Here it is the six-syllable mantra of Avalokiteshvara, *Om mani padme hum*, which you recite for a "mala," or one round of the 108 beads of the rosary, or as many times as you can. As we will see in the later chapters on highest yoga tantra, reciting a mantra is much more than silently mumbling a few Sanskrit syllables. A mantra is "that which protects the mind" as we saw when we looked at the name Mantrayana as an alternate name for Vajrayana. Used in conjunction with the visualization of yourself as the deity, or a front-generation deity, combined with an understanding of emptiness, mantra recitation is a vital part of the process of transforming the ordinary, deluded mind to an extra-ordinary, pure one.

Mantra recitation involves purification of the speech as well as the mind, and therefore it is recommended some of the recitation at least should be aloud. In effect, what that usually involves is starting by quietly saying the mantra and then later allowing it to become a sound in the head. In highest yoga tantra, there are many more levels of subtlety in mantra recitation, and a kriya tantra practice is in some ways a preparation for this.

After the recitation of the main mantra, there is a Vajrasattva purification mantra, common at the end of most sadhanas to purify any mistakes made doing the sadhana. Mistakes and slips of concentration have definitely occurred during the practice, and there are many methods you can use to purify this, but the hundred-syllable Vajrasattva mantra, or even the short one, is considered supreme. People wanting to do extensive purification are often advised to do a three-month Vajrasattva retreat where 100,000 mantras are recited. This is considered extremely powerful. Lama Zopa Rinpoche recommends doing at least twenty-one mantras at the end of each day, which effectively purifies any negative karma at all accumulated during the day.

Many sadhanas then describe the reemergence of the deity. If you are doing a front generation, the threefold stack arises atop a moon and lotus back in the space in front of you. If you have received the full initiation (*wang* or oral transmission) into Four-Arm Avalokiteshvara or a full initiation into a highest yoga tantra meditation cycle with a subsequent permission (*jenang*) for Four-Arm Avalokiteshvara, you would do a self-generation at this point. Self-generation, again, is where you visualize that you yourself arise as the deity out of emptiness. *Inseparability* is not explicit on this.

Finally there are concluding prayers and the dedication of whatever merit was gained from the practice. These final aspirations can be supplemented with other prayers as desired, such as with long-life prayers for your teachers.

Pranayama

As we've seen, another important aspect of kriya tantra sadhanas is the practice of *pranayama*, or "subduing the vital wind." We looked at this in the previous chapter where we discussed the differences between the practices of this name in kriya tantra and in highest yoga tantra, but it may be helpful to take a closer look at what this practice entails for kriya tantra.

The goal is to have a clear visualization of the deity, moon disc, and mantra garland. At present when we try to meditate the mind refuses to remain on the object of meditation. As we have seen, the mind rides on the wind energies, and it is this that we are trying to tame. Rather than allowing the mind to move from one object to another whenever it wants as it normally does, we must learn to subdue it and keep it still. When that is achieved, strong concentration and vivid visualizations are easy.

Having cleansed the three main channels using the nine-point breathing briefly discussed in chapter 3, you can now actually hold the breath using what is called *vase breathing*, the most important part of pranayama. This is done by holding the breath from above and below and trapping it at a point just below the navel, like water trapped within the confines of a vase. From above, hold your breath as you do when you dive in water—you simply stop breathing. From below, tense the muscles around your bowels and pelvis, thus creating a sort of tension that traps the wind energy in that area.

Then, visualize the upper energy—the vital wind that controls the upper part of your body—descending to that point, and the lower energy—that which controls the lower part of your body—ascending to that point, concentrating all your vital wind into a bubble or vase of energy.

Hold the breath as long as you can—how long will vary for each person—while reciting the mantra and visualizing the deity, moon disc, and mantra garland. When you cannot hold your breath any longer, exhale. When you relax like this you should simply bring your mind to the visualization of the deity, nothing more. Then, as you release the energy with the out-breath, the mind can naturally focus on the deity.

There are several steps of increasing subtlety in this practice. They are:

+ recitation focusing on the front-generation deity
+ recitation on the mind at the heart of the front-generation deity
+ recitation on the mind at one's own heart

+ recitation focusing on the form of the mantra
+ recitation of the mind focusing on the sound of the mantra

The first part of the meditation is called the *recitation focusing on the front-generation deity*. Here, you remain focused on the deity until you are ready to do another round of vase breathing. Then repeat the process: breathing in, holding the breath, tensing the muscles, reciting the mantra, and visualizing the three elements of deity, moon disc, and mantra.

This can be hard work, so it's not a good idea to do this meditation for too long when your practice is new. While you are resting, continue to say the mantra and hold the visualization of the front-generation deity.

Then, when you feel ready, you can take the meditation to the next stage, the *recitation on the mind at the heart of the front-generation deity*. Here, at the resting stage, rather than just visualizing the deity, you concentrate on the moon disc at the deity's heart and the mantra garland that sits on the moon disc.

With the third round, the *recitation on the mind at one's own heart*, you focus your mind on the moon disc and the mantra garland at your own heart.

The next stage is called the *recitation focusing on the form of the mantra*. This visualization is done while holding your breath rather than during the resting periods between the vase breathing. Visualize that the moon disc and mantra at the front-generation deity's heart rise, exit the deity's mouth, and enter your nostrils as you take an in-breath, moving to your own heart. Holding that visualization in place, do the vase breathing. You should always breathe through the nostrils so you can feel the moon disc and mantra from the front-generation deity come in through your nostrils with that breath. While holding the breath at the navel, focus the visualization at the heart and say the mantra until you need to release your breath.

The final round is called the *recitation of the mind focusing on the sound of the mantra.* Here you move from the visualization of the mantra to the sound of the mantra; otherwise the procedure is exactly the same. It should not seem like you are listening to the mantra being recited by people outside of you somewhere. Rather the mantra should be resonating in your heart as a pure and natural sound.

A Passport to a New Universe

This is the power of Vajrayana. The practice includes both deep concentration and a profound understanding of emptiness based on the foundation of the altruistic wish to attain enlightenment for the benefit of others. The whole of the Buddhist path is there within a sadhana. This is where Vajrayana is unique. The Sutrayana has practices to develop calm abiding, and these are done in parallel with separate practices to develop compassion, which are in turn separate from the practices to develop an understanding of emptiness. All that is included within one Vajrayana practice, within one sadhana.

The sadhana is like a passport to a new universe. At first glance it may seem like an arcane ritual, but when we understand the skillful way it can transform the mind, and especially how it uniquely blends the conventional aspects of our practice, such as developing the altruistic mind, with the wisdom realizing emptiness, we can see what a profound psychological tool it is. Each deity in Tibetan Vajrayana is an iconic representation of a particular enlightened energy within us that we are trying to actualize. As Lama Govinda says in *The Way of the White Clouds*:

[The tantric deity images] were not merely beautiful decorations of aesthetic value but representations of a higher reality, born from visions of inner experience. They were put into as precise a language of forms as is contained in a geographical map or a scientific formula, while being as natural in expression and as direct in appeal as a flower or a sunset.[23]

5 Preparation for Highest Yoga Tantra

The Many Deities within Vajrayana

WITH AN UNDERSTANDING of the essential elements of kriya tantra, we can now move toward an examination of highest yoga tantra practice. There are some elements of kriya, charya, and yoga tantric teachings present in Korean, Japanese, and Chinese Buddhism, but Tibetan Buddhism is the only form of Buddhism to practice highest yoga tantra. Thus it is a singular subject of study and practice.

Within Tibetan Buddhism there are four schools or traditions: Nyingma, Sakya, Kagyu, and Gelug. There are not many differences in the way these schools study and practice the Sutrayana. Where they differ is in their practice of highest yoga tantra, and within it, which tantra and tantric deity they emphasize.

My explanation follows the Gelug tradition of Lama Tsongkhapa. Although there are several deities practiced in this tradition, the three main deities practiced are Guhyasamaja, Yamantaka, and Heruka Chakrasamvara. His Holiness the Dalai Lama also often gives the Kalachakra initiation to thousands of people as an important focus for developing world peace, and these days female deities such as Vajrayogini and Chittamani Tara are often practiced, too. The choice of tantric deity to be practiced is in the hands of the practitioner and his or her teacher, who will advise which is the most suitable.

Within highest yoga tantra, there are three types of tantras: father tantra, mother tantra, and nondual tantra. They differ in whether they name the realization of the illusory body or the realization of the clear light as the most crucial step toward enlightenment. According to Lama Tsongkhapa, father tantra—also called *method tantra*—is the category of highest yoga tantras that emphasizes the attainment of enlightenment through the realization of the illusory body, while mother tantra, or *wisdom tantra*, emphasizes clear light. In nondual tantra, method and wisdom are equally important. *Method* refers here not to conventional bodhichitta but to pristine cognition (Skt. *jñana*; Tib. *yeshe*), or the union of great bliss and wisdom realizing emptiness. Guhyasamaja tantra is a father tantra.

Traditionally, the Guhyasamaja system is used in the Gelug tradition to explain the processes used within a highest yoga tantra sadhana, including the chakras, channels, winds, and drops, and that is the tantra I will use as my template. That is not to say it is superior or preferable to other highest yoga tantra practices. I am using Guhyasamaja because I personally have had instructions on it, and so it is the one I feel most confident to try to explain. Its emphasis on the practice of taking ordinary death, intermediate state, and rebirth into the path as the three *kayas*, or buddha bodies, is particularly useful. If you already practice another highest yoga tantra deity, you will find similarities and differences, but hopefully by following the explanations in the next chapters you will gain a good understanding of the whole mechanism of highest yoga tantra and what it aims to achieve, which is enlightenment itself.

An Overview of the Generation Stage

The main objective of highest yoga tantra is to move the subtle winds or energies through the central channel to eventually enter the heart chakra and abide there. When all of the subtle winds are dissolved into the indestructible drop at the heart chakra, we experience the clear-light mind. When the clear-light mind eventually comes into union with the illusory body, the resultant state—enlightenment—is achieved.

In the generation stage, we prepare our mind for this transformation through meditation by visualizing the process of dissolving the winds into the central channel in different stages and imagining what the mind experiences at each different stage. In other words, the final three generation-stage meditations of experiencing the clear-light mind, the illusory body, and the union of clear light and illusory body are very profound meditations, but they are still only happening at an imaginary level. At this point in our practice, we can only impute what will actually happen in the completion stage, so the generation stage is also called the *imputed stage* or the *contrived stage*. The concentration required to actually move the subtle winds of the body into the central channel is enormous. There is no way any meditator could practice the completion stage without a firm training in the generation stage; hence this stage is also called the *yoga of the first stage*.

In *Paths and Grounds of Guhyasamaja* by Yangchen Gawai Lodoe, the generation stage is defined as:

> ...a yoga that is a meditation that accords with any of the aspects of death, intermediate state, or rebirth. It is also a factor for ripening the mental continuum for its resultant state, the completion stage, not arising through the actual meditation practice of the winds entering, abiding, and dissolving in the central channel.[24]

This definition shows us three vital aspects of a generation-stage practice. The most important thing is that the generation stage is a preparation for the completion stage, maturing the mind so it is ready for the process of actually moving the winds into the central channel. The second point is that this movement is not a feature of the generation stage itself. The third aspect is that the various generation-stage practices "accord" with ordinary death, intermediate state, and rebirth, which means that we mimic these stages of passing from this life to another and hence familiarize ourselves with the clear-light mind of death, the mind we will use in the completion stage to attain enlightenment. Kirti Tsenshap Rinpoche in his *Principles of Buddhist Tantra* explains that these three aspects are only found in the main father tantras of Guhyasamaja and Yamantaka. All highest yoga tantra generation-stages practice, however, are a preparation for the completion stage.

PREPARATION FOR PRACTICING THE GENERATION STAGE

Meditating on death, intermediate state, and rebirth is not unique to highest yoga tantra. Understanding these phenomena is a crucial aspect of any Buddhist path; meditation on death is particularly prevalent across Buddhism, from Sutrayana to highest yoga tantra. In Sutrayana these meditations are done to realize the fundamentally impermanent nature of our lives. In the preparation for generation-stage practice, the goal is to also understand what actually happens when death occurs. We are asked to experience through our imagination exactly what it is like to go through the death process and to feel the experiences that a dying person has, the mental states that are passed through, particularly at death's final stage.

We need to be similarly aware of the intermediate state, or *bardo*: the process of entering the intermediate state after death, what an intermediate-state being experiences, and what happens as the being passes from the intermediate state into the next rebirth. We need to understand the way the gross consciousnesses dissolve at death, and conversely how the subtle consciousnesses become grosser with the birth process. This practice is crucial to the generation stage; it provides vital training for the completion stage, where we can actually take the processes of dying, becoming an intermediate-state being, and taking rebirth and use them to attain enlightenment, either through meditation or at the time of our own natural death. Either way, the method is extraordinary and the result is extraordinary.

During a naturally occurring process of death, intermediate state, and rebirth, a person's mental state changes. As the mind goes through what are called the *dissolutions*, it transforms from gross to subtle to even more subtle until, at the moment of death, it becomes the very basic subtle mind, which in highest yoga tantra is often called the *base clear light*. This refers to the clear-light mind that is naturally there all the time but only manifests at the time of death.

When a person enters the intermediate state, the mind reverts from the subtlest mind of clear light to a grosser mind—although not as gross as the ordinary types of minds we have now—and then moves back to the subtler mind again. At that stage, the intermediate-state being has a body, although it is a mental body, not a physical one. When rebirth occurs, the subtle mind of the intermediate-state being becomes grosser and grosser until it becomes the gross consciousness that we experience in our daily life.

These gross and subtle consciousnesses move on wind energies that are able to pass into the normally blocked central channel and enter the heart chakra. This happens naturally at the time of death, but normally it goes by so quickly; we have no awareness or control of the process, and the force of our previous karma and habits pushes us through it and on into the next life with no lasting benefit. In tantra, we try and get the winds to dissolve in the central channel while we are still alive so that we can use it as a staging ground for buddhahood. Thus it is extremely useful to practice being able to manipulate the winds in the generation stage. By the time we have reached the completion stage, through continued practice we will be able to actually emulate what naturally happens at death.

In other words, we make it happen by meditation. We are actually able to move the subtle winds into the central channel so they eventually reach the center of the heart chakra to enter, abide, and dissolve there, and through that dissolution we experience the clear-light mind and then the union of that clear-light mind and illusory body. In this way it is possible to attain enlightenment in this same lifetime.

Even if we are not able to do this during our lifetime, we may be able to do it during our actual death. If we have trained in highest yoga tantra and developed great meditation skills, it is possible to stay in meditation through the entire natural death process. We can control what happens when the winds move into the central channel naturally. Rather than allowing the subtle wind at the moment of death to move the mind into the intermediate state, we can instead turn it into the illusory body and then bring the clear-light mind and the illusory body together, and thereby attain enlightenment at that time.

Death, Intermediate State, and Rebirth

THE EIGHT DISSOLUTIONS OF ORDINARY DEATH

Sometimes you see statements in the sadhanas like "taking death as the dharmakaya." This is the title of a particular meditation, but it is a little misleading. It does not mean you imagine your death. The process of death, intermediate state, and rebirth has already become familiar before we start the generation-stage meditation. The meditation parallels the death process; it does not replicate it. Just as in ordinary death, the mind becomes more and more subtle and various elements dissolve, in our meditation we visualize the various deities that reside in our body dissolving, representing particular constituents, such as the body, feeling, and so forth. That particular deity or group of deities dissolves, and with that dissolution we have a particular experience.

Even though every tantra is slightly different in the details of the dissolutions, each is the same in correlating to the actual process of death, intermediate state, and rebirth.

In the ordinary death process, the mind becomes more and more subtle, and its grosser elements can no longer manifest. That means that the dying person quickly loses the sense faculties and conscious thoughts that make up our normal everyday experience. This process happens in eight main stages, where various elements cease to function. These are called the *eight dissolutions*.

In the early dissolutions, the aspect of the body that is losing strength is represented by one of the four natural elements—earth, water, fire, or wind. The earth element is the physical aspects of our body, or our flesh and bones; water is the liquid aspects of our body, or our blood, saliva, urine, and so forth; fire is the heat of our body; and wind is the various winds that control our movement.

The dissolutions are also related to the five primordial wisdoms: the dharmadhatu wisdom (or the wisdom of natural phenomena), the mirror-like wisdom, the wisdom of equality, the wisdom of analysis, and the wisdom of achieving activities. Although there are different interpretations on the meaning of the five primordial wisdoms, we can think of them like this. The dharmadhatu wisdom is the mind of bare nonconceptualizing awareness; the mirror-like wisdom is the mind devoid of dualistic thought, "like a mirror and its reflections"; the wisdom of equality is the mind that sees the universe as one taste in emptiness; the wisdom of analysis perceives the uniqueness of each and every phenomenon; and the wisdom of achieving activities is the mind that spontaneously works for the welfare of others. We each of us have these five primordial wisdoms to some degree—the ability to differentiate many objects without confusion, a sense of equality in some areas (although we are biased in others), the ability to analyze, and so forth—and it is this that diminishes and ceases as we die.

And so with the first dissolution, the earth element—the sense of corporeality—loses strength as it dissolves into the water element. It is not that the fluid aspect of the body becomes stronger; rather it becomes more manifest with the weakening of the earth element. The dying person's limbs become very thin and loose, but she has an external feeling of great heaviness as if her body were sinking under the earth. This is the dissolution of the form aggregate, the body. The body becomes weak and powerless; its luster diminishes. The person's eye sense becomes weak, and she can no longer open or close her eyes or distinguish colors and shapes. Everything appears dark and indistinct. Of the five primordial wisdoms, the basic mirror-like wisdom, the ability to perceive many things simultaneously, is lost here first. Each dissolution is also accompanied by an internal sign. For the first dissolution it is the appearance of a mirage, like shimmering water.

With the second dissolution, the water element dissolves into the fire element. The water element becomes weaker and deteriorates, and whatever moisture there is in the body—in the form of saliva, sweat, or urine—dries up. The aggregate of feeling is lost, and so the dying person is no longer conscious of the feelings of pleasure, pain, and neutrality that usually accompany any sensory experience. The basic wisdom that is lost is the wisdom of equality. The sense that dissolves is hearing, so she can no longer hear either external or internal sounds. The internal sign is the appearance of smoke.

With the third dissolution, the fire element—the heat in the body—becomes weaker, allowing the wind element to become more manifest. The dying person can no longer remember the names of the people close to her, and she is no longer conscious of what is happening around her. The aggregate of discrimination and the basic wisdom of analysis falter. Her nose sense weakens, and she can no longer smell things or digest food and drink. The internal sign is the appearance of sparks.

Next, with the fourth dissolution, the last of the four elements, the wind element, dissolves. The external sign is that the ten winds move into the heart, and the dying person stops breathing. She can no longer perform any functions at all, as the aggregate of compositional factors dissolves and the tongue and body senses are lost. The tongue becomes thick, and she can no longer experience smoothness and roughness or experience tastes and tangible objects. With the dissolution of the basic wisdom of achieving activities, she is no longer mindful of external worldly activities. The internal sign is like a butter lamp sputtering out.

The dying person has stopped breathing, but the mind has not stopped functioning. She is clinically dead, but according to Buddhism, the moment of death, when the mind disassociates from the body, has not yet arrived. First more dissolutions must occur.

With the fifth dissolution, the eighty grosser conceptions dissolve, triggering the winds in the right and left channels above the heart to move into the central channel at the top of the head. The basic wisdom of the dharmadhatu is lost. The internal sign is a moving from the sputtering butter lamp, as in the previous dissolution, to a clear vacuity filled with white light. This is also sometimes described as an appearance like moonlight in an autumn sky. It is called the *white appearance*.

Now, with the sixth dissolution, it is time for the lower winds that reside in the right and left channels below the heart to enter the central channel at the base of the spine. This triggers a vision of the white vacuity becoming a clear vacuity filled with red light, caused by the dissolution of the winds carrying the white-appearance consciousness. This is sometimes described as a sunset in a clear autumn sky and is called the *red increase*.

With the seventh dissolution, the winds that carry the red increase dissolve into the winds that carry the mind, which experiences the *black near-attainment*. Thus the internal sign is moving from the red vision to an appearance of thick darkness and then a sense of swooning, of becoming unconscious.

Finally with the eighth dissolution, the moment of death arrives, as all the winds dissolve into the very subtle life-bearing wind in the indestructible drop at the heart. It is as if the consciousness arises from the swoon of the last dissolution and enters the clear light of death.[25]

THE ORDINARY INTERMEDIATE STATE

Between this life and the next is the intermediate state, or *bardo*.[26] Only beings who are going to be born in the formless realms[27] do not experience the intermediate state. For them, when the actual death occurs, they move from the clear light straight to the next rebirth. For everyone else, after the clear light of death occurs, that clear-light mind acts as the cooperative cause to bring about the mind of an intermediate-state being, and the wind or energy that carries the clear light acts as the main or substantial cause of the intermediate-state body.

As soon as this happens, the death process starts to reverse. The first stage after the clear light is the black near-attainment; this is when the intermediate-state being actually comes into existence as the karma of the previous body is finished and a new body is established. Although we call it a "body," it is not a physical body but a wind body, in that it comes from the two causes of the wind that carries the clear light and the clear light itself. After black near-attainment, the other appearances follow, in the opposite order of the eight dissolutions: red increase, white appearance, the appearance like a sputtering butter lamp, the appearance like fireflies, the appearance like smoke, and the appearance like a mirage.

The intermediate-state being is sometimes called "spontaneously born" because all of its faculties and limbs come together spontaneously in the same moment. Because the being is searching for its next rebirth in the intermediate state, it can be known as a "seeker of existence." And it is sometimes called a "smell eater" because its main food is smell.

The intermediate-state being is said to arise from the mind because its body does not come from the mother's egg and father's sperm. Wherever this being travels, there are no physical obstructions like mountains or walls. It can see its previous body, home, and environment, but it can only be seen by other intermediate-state beings and people with some kind of clairvoyance.

The physical appearance of the intermediate-state being is directly related to the birth it will take. For example, if it is going to be born as a human, the being will have all the features of a human. An intermediate-state being destined to be born in the lower realms has a dark appearance, like that of a tree trunk burnt by fire for a hell being or having the color of water for a hungry ghost. One destined for a fortunate rebirth has an appearance like moonlight.

The orientation of its body as it travels from one place to another also depends on its next rebirth. If it is going to be born in the lower realms, it travels upside down with its head down and legs up. An intermediate-state being who is going to be born in the upper realms as a human being or a desire-realm god moves horizontally. Beings destined to be born in the form realm move in an upright position.

The lifespan of the intermediate-state being is seven days. If it has not taken rebirth in that time, it will experience what is called a *small death* and then be born again in the intermediate state. This can happen up to seven times, so the being will have found its next corporeal body within forty-nine days.

As we have seen, the shape of the intermediate-state being is an indication of its rebirth. But can it escape that fate and experience a different rebirth? According to the *Treasury of Higher Knowledge* (*Abhidharmakosha*), the text by the great scholar Vasubandhu, the being will inevitably take rebirth in the realm indicated by its body. However, Asanga, in his *Compendium of Higher Knowledge* (*Abhidharma-samucchaya*), asserts that it is possible to change the realm of rebirth if the being or its relatives can generate enough strong virtue.

THE ORDINARY REBIRTH

To understand how the consciousness leaves the intermediate state and takes rebirth, we will look at the process as it is described in the *Entering into the Womb Sutra* (*Garbhavakranti Sutra*). The sutra describes three favorable conditions that need to be present and three obstacles that need to be absent for a being to move to the next life, such as the future father and mother being in sexual union and there being no deformity to the womb or the woman not having a period.

If all these conditions are met, the intermediate-state being, having a close karmic connection to the future parents, sees them engaged in sexual intercourse and, while the mother's 72,000 channels are filled with pleasure from the sexual act, enters the womb of the mother either through the mouth or the crown. An intermediate-state being who is going to be born as a male has a strong sense of dislike toward the father but attachment to the mother; one with a female rebirth will have a strong dislike for the mother but attachment to the father.

The combination of that aversion and attachment acts to end the intermediate-state existence, forcing the being to move from the intermediate state to its next rebirth. When that happens, the death process starts to occur in the same order as in a natural death—starting with appearances like a mirage, smoke, and fireflies, up to black near-attainment dissolving into clear light. That consciousness of clear light enters the mother's womb, and then the reverse order starts, from the clear light to black near-attainment up to the appearance like a mirage.

With the coming together of the sperm and egg, the embryo is formed from two substances, the white substance from the father and the red one from the mother.

Initially the fetus is covered in what looks and feels like cream, while the inside is still liquid. Then, both outside and inside slowly solidify, going from a jelly-like substance to one that has the resilience and elasticity of meat. At each of these stages, a new wind forms, causing further development. During the fourth week, the white and red drops divide into refined and unrefined drops. From the white drops develop the three aspects from the father of regenerative fluid, marrow, and bone, and from the red drops develop the three aspects from the mother of flesh, skin, and blood.

Then, slowly, the fetus develops, with the body taking shape, the limbs and head forming and the sense organs developing. With that, the sense faculties develop. After these stages, the length of time the child stays in the mother's womb and its positions during those nine months indicate whether it will be a son or daughter.

Although it is not necessary to understand all the processes involved in our ordinary death, intermediate state, and rebirth, it is a great help to our practice in seeing how these three stages are mimicked in the highest yoga tantra practice of taking them as the three buddha bodies.

The Four Levels of Achievement

There are various levels of attainment we progress through in our generation-stage practice. Although there is no clear demarcation between one level and the next, or even between the end of our generation-stage practice and the beginning of the completion stage, it helps to see what stages our practice passes through.

In general, the generation stage is divided into *coarse yoga* and *subtle yoga*. Starting with visualizations that are very imprecise and that fluctuate in strength, clarity, and detail, we progress to the more advanced subtle-yoga stage, where we can hold very detailed visualizations of each of the deities and the entire mandala at the same time. These two levels correspond to four levels of achievement which are:

+ beginner's level
+ slight dawning of wisdom
+ slight control over wisdom
+ perfect control over wisdom

The first two levels correspond to the coarse yoga and the latter two to the subtle yoga. At the *beginner's level,* our focus is on understanding the structure of the sadhana. We shouldn't worry about holding the entire visualization at one time—that would be impossible at this stage anyway. We imagine the deities as quite big, and when the sadhana describes Guhyasamaja's face, we concentrate on that; when it describes a hand, we move to that; and so forth. This does not mean that our visualizations are weak, however; if the mandala has thirty-two deities, we must have a very powerful visualization to be able to imagine all thirty-two!

The visualization of the mandala during the coarse-yoga stage is sometimes called the *overview yoga of the coarse-generation stage.* This is because during this stage we focus strongly on the mandala, building up a mental image of the mandala, its various deities, and their ornaments and features. At this point the main focus is the bigger picture. We build up all the parts of the deities and the mandala step by step rather than focusing on the tiny details like the deities at the sense organs, which is done later in the subtle-yoga stage.

At this level we are not allowed to break the sadhana in the middle. We must follow it all the way to the end, and we may be asked to do so several times in one day. This is so we can get a good sense of the entire practice and build up the various elements of the visualization to understand how they fit together.

By the second level, the *slight dawning of wisdom*, the latter part of the coarse-yoga stage, we can hold the visualization of the deity and the mandala for a whole day. At the beginner's level, these things were built up step by step. Here we can hold the entire visualization at the same time with some degree of clarity for an extended period of time, but we are still unable to clearly visualize the subtle elements of the deities and the mandalas, such as the tiny deities residing in the sense organs of the principal deity or the intricate details of the decorations of the mandala.

When we have reached the third stage, *slight control over wisdom*, we can visualize the mandala and the principal deity easily and instantaneously. We can also hold the tiny deities and the intricate decorations of the mandala with great clarity. For example, the principal deity of the Guhyasamaja mandala has various deities at each sense organ and joint. At this stage, we are able to visualize all of these deities on the principal deity vividly. Unlike the first two levels, where we hold a fairly large visualization, now we can hold this visualization in all its detail within the size of a tiny drop.

The name "slight control over wisdom" refers to the ability to visualize the deity and mandala created from the wisdom realizing emptiness. The conjoining of the perfect concentration of calm abiding with the special insight analyzing emptiness is a crucial factor in progressing through the latter stages of highest yoga tantra, and here we are not only able to realize emptiness, but we are also becoming skilled at developing both calm abiding and special insight simultaneously. This is called the "union of calm abiding and special insight through deity yoga conjoined with great bliss and emptiness."

When we can do the visualization within an extremely small space, visualizing the deities and the entire mandala inside a sesame seed, we are practicing subtle yoga. This stage is also known as *the yoga of supreme detail*. Yangchen Gawai Lodoe describes the capabilities of a practitioner of this stage:

> Within a spot of light on the tip of the nose, a practitioner can visualize both the mandala and its residents.[28]

At the fourth level, *perfect control over wisdom*, we have realized emptiness through experiencing the clear light, which is the antidote to the obscurations to liberation.[29] Through meditation, the winds will enter, abide, and dissolve into the central channel, ultimately causing the clear light to occur. That clear light realizes emptiness, but not as yet directly. Although this fourth level of achievement is technically included in the generation stage, if we have reached this level then we have probably already commenced the completion stage.

6 PRACTICING THE GENERATION STAGE

EVERY TANTRIC DEITY is practiced differently, and every practice is incredibly complex. Rather than trying to explain all the practices and how they differ, I have chosen one Guhyasamaja sadhana to use as an example.[30] This sadhana is a representative and complete father-tantra practice, so you will be able to take what is here and use it to understand your own practice regardless of its deity.

Before the Actual Practice

As with the kriya tantra practice, in highest yoga tantra there are many activities that need to be done before we do the actual practice. In this case, the preliminary practices are the yoga of taking death, intermediate state, and rebirth as the three bodies into the path. In a long sadhana such as the extended Guhyasamaja sadhana, this stage is divided into two sections: beginning the session, and the main preliminary practice.

The practices that begin the session are done in five stages:

- ✦ generating oneself into the deity
- ✦ blessing the vajra and bell and the inner offering
- ✦ offering the preliminary *torma* (ritual cake)

+ blessing the self-generation's offering
+ practicing Vajrasattva

First we generate ourselves as the deity. With devotion to the direct and indirect lineage masters, we make a strong prayer, through which we arise in the deity's form. In the case of the Guhyasamaja sadhana, the self-generation Guhyasamaja is called Krodhavajra with consort Sparshavajra. We should have not just a vivid and clear visualization but also a very strong divine identity as the deity.

Then we bless the vajra and bell and the inner offering. There are many different ways of blessing the vajra and bell, but here it is mainly done by remembering that the vajra signifies the method side of the practice and the bell signifies the wisdom side. Then we bless the inner offering. The inner offering is made up of the five meats, representing the five afflictive elements—of earth (solidity), water (fluidity), fire (heat), air (motility), and space—and the five nectars, representing the five contaminated aggregates. The five meats and the five nectars are visualized as impure substances, such as rotting flesh or urine, held in a vast skull cup, or *kapala*. After purifying these substances into pure ones, we make the blessing.

We cleanse the substances by reciting the action mantra, *Om ah vighnantakrit hum*, remembering that the substances are empty of inherent existence. By repeating the emptiness mantra, *Om shunyata jñana vajra svabhava atmako ham*, all the substances in the inner offering turn into clear light.

We then offer the preliminary *torma* (Skt. *bali*) offering. A *torma* is a ritual cake offered to the deities. After blessing the six or seven offerings on our altar, we offer the actual torma itself as a separate offering. We invoke the protectors of the ten directions,[31] presenting the torma offering and making requests to them.

Next we bless the self-generation's offering. Again, with the understanding of emptiness, we cleanse the offerings by saying the action mantra and purifying them with the emptiness mantra (*Om shun-yata...*). From a syllable *ah* arise skull cups, inside of which are offerings, each offering marked by the first letter of its Sanskrit name. Then with strong concentration, we say the mantra of each offering while doing its mudra. This is also done for the blessing of the preliminary offering and the preliminary torma. Finally, we do a short Vajrasattva practice in order to purify any negativities. This is a standard element of all highest yoga tantra meditation manuals.

Having completed these practices, we can move to the main preliminary practices, which consist of:

+ the seven-limb prayer
+ meditating on ultimate protection
+ meditating on the protection wheel

We have already seen the *seven-limb prayer* in our kriya yoga sadhana; this is a very common practice for Tibetan Buddhists. *Meditating on ultimate protection* means generating a mind of emptiness and developing a strong sense of divine identity. *Meditating on the protection wheel* means visualizing the central deity and retinue and visualizing a fence made of vajras as a protection. When these preliminary practices are finished, we can move to the main body of the practice.

The Three Components of the Guhyasamaja Sadhana

The generation-stage practice within the Guhyasamaja sadhana has three components:

+ meditative absorption on the initial engagement
+ meditative absorption on the supreme victorious mandala
+ meditative absorption on the supreme activities

The practice is not complete without all three components, but the first section, *meditative absorption on the initial engagement*, is the most important in helping us understand the process a meditator goes through during the generation stage. Thus it will be our primary focus here.

The main practice within this component is the three yogas:

+ the yoga of taking death as dharmakaya into the path
+ the yoga of taking the bardo as sambhogakaya into the path
+ the yoga of taking rebirth as nirmanakaya into the path

The first step is to visualize the principal deity (in this case, Guhyasamaja) and the surrounding thirty-two deities within the mandala palace. The entire mandala, including its deities, is supposed to appear instantaneously, but of course, while we are new to the practice we will need to slowly build this image up.

Once we have firmly established the mandala and deities, we withdraw all the deities to various places in our body—Vairochana to our crown, Lochana to our navel, and so forth—which here again is not visualized as our ordinary, flawed body but as the body of the deity. Each of the thirty-two deities represents a different aspect of our deity's form, either an aspect of the physical body, a mental state, or a particular energy. This process is known as the *withdrawal of the special imagined deities into the body*.

This visualization is incredibly complex, with each deity possessing a different location, appearance, and significance. These are listed in table 2.

The sun and moon cushions of the front-generation visualization are also withdrawn if we are not going to do an extensive practice. However, if we are, then they are left inside the mandala for a later visualization practice that comes under the second heading, the meditative absorption on the supreme victorious mandala. By visualizing

TABLE 2. THE THIRTY-TWO DEITIES OF GUHYASAMAJA

DEITY	COLOR	LOCATION	SIGNIFICANCE
Vairochana	white	crown to the hairline	reality of the form aggregate
Amitabha	red	hairline to the throat	reality of the compositional factors aggregate
Akshobhya	blue	throat to the heart	reality of the consciousness aggregate
Ratnasambhava	yellow	heart to the navel	reality of the feeling aggregate
Amoghasiddhi	green	navel to the groin	reality of the discrimination aggregate
Lochana	white	navel	earth element
Mamaki	blue	heart	water element
Pandaravasini	red	throat	fire element
Tara	green	crown	air element
Kshitigarbha	white	eyes	reality of the eye organs
Rupavajra	white	doors of the eyes	reality of visual forms
Vajrapani	yellow	ears	reality of the ear organs
Shaptavajra	yellow	doors of the ears	reality of sound
Akashagarbha	yellow	nose	reality of the nose organ
Gandhavajra	red	door of the nose	reality of the sense of smell
Lokeshvara	red	tongue	reality of the tongue sense
Rasavajra	green	door of the mouth	reality of taste
Manjushri	red	heart	reality of the mind or mental sense
Sarvanivaranavishkambhini	green	door of the vajra	reality of the body organ
Sparshavajra	blue	door of the vajra	reality of textures
Samantabhadra	green	joints	reality of the joints
Maitreya	white	crown	reality of the nerves and sinews
Yamantaka	black	right hand	reality of HUM
Aparajita	white	left hand	reality of HUM
Hayagriva	red	mouth	reality of HUM
Vighnantaka	black	vajra	reality of HUM
Achala	black	right shoulder nerve	reality of HUM
Takkiraja	black	left shoulder nerve	reality of HUM
Niladanda	blue	right knee	reality of HUM
Mahabala	blue	left knee	reality of HUM
Ushinishachakravartin	blue	crown	reality of HUM
Sumbharaja	blue	soles of the feet	reality of HUM

the deities in this way, we are setting up the visualization in preparation for the main part of the practice—the dissolution of all these deities until the dharmakaya is attained, which mirrors the death process; reestablishing ourselves as the deity in the sambhogakaya aspect, mirroring the ordinary bardo process; and finally reestablishing ourselves in the nirmanakaya aspect, mirroring ordinary rebirth, where we can do activities for all sentient beings.

The Yoga of Taking Death as the Dharmakaya into the Path

THE EIGHT DISSOLUTIONS

As we saw in the last chapter, in the ordinary death process the eight dissolutions occur as each element weakens, allowing the next element to become more manifest. In the meditation on the yoga of taking death as the dharmakaya into the path, we mimic this. Here, as the Guhyasamaja sadhana states, the deities that we have visualized in our body "dissolve into clear light in sequence." Each set of deities represents a particular element, and each set dissolves with that element's dissolution.

In a natural death, we actually experience each of the dissolutions. In this meditation, we visualize the elements dissolving and recite the names of the deities associated with those elements as we simultaneously visualize those deities dissolving into clear light. With the last dissolution, the principal and the consort dissolve, which gives rise to the clear-light mind.

And so in the first dissolution, when the earth element dissolves and we have the vision of a mirage, the first set of deities, from Vairochana to Achala, each dissolve in sequence. These deities are the essence of what we naturally are—the earth element, the aggregate of form, the eye sense, the perception of color and shape, and so forth. In the actual death, these elements are said to cease their functions, but here the manual says that the deities in the nature of those elements and aggregates "dissolve."

In the same way, we go through the other dissolutions, with the deities dissolving in sequence, as depicted in table 3.

At the eighth dissolution, the principal deity dissolves with the consort, bringing the clear-light mind. Although called the mind of the clear light of death, this is not the same clear light that occurs at the time of our ordinary death. The clear-light mind of this stage is defined by three characteristics:

+ It has realized emptiness.
+ It experiences great bliss.
+ It has the feeling of vastness or being empty.

With this clear mind we think, "This is my resultant state of dharmakaya."

At the generation stage, this thought can purify our ordinary death. The clear-light mind occurs naturally at the time of death, but if we have a longstanding generation-stage practice, it is possible to hold this meditation during the death process and realize emptiness as we die, actually feeling great bliss and having the sensation of vastness. In this sense, visualizing the eight dissolutions is merely preparation for the real meditation, which is the visualization of the dharmakaya that we will achieve upon becoming a buddha.

THE BASE, PATH, AND RESULT IN THE DEATH PRACTICE

In Buddhism, the terms *base*, *path*, and *result* are commonly used to show where we start, what we do, and what our goal is. In this practice, our ordinary death is the *base*, the *path* is the process that can bring about states of mind that can actually purify our ordinary death,

Table 3. The eight dissolutions

Factor	External Sign	Internal Deities	Deities Dissolving
First dissolution			
earth element dissolves	Body becomes very thin, limbs loose; there is the sense that the body is sinking under the earth.	appearance of mirage	Vairochana
			Lochana
			Kshitigarbha
aggregate of form dissolves	Limbs become smaller; body becomes weak and powerless; the luster of your body diminishes; your strength is consumed.		Rupavajra
			Maitreya
eye sense dissolves	You cannot open or close your eyes, and colors and shapes are lost. Your sight becomes unclear and dark.		Yamantaka
			Achala
basic mirror-like wisdom dissolves	The ordinary consciousness that clearly perceives many objects simultaneously.		
Second dissolution			
water element dissolves	Saliva, sweat, urine, blood, and regenerative fluid dry greatly.	appearance of smoke	Ratnasambhava
			Mamaki
aggregate of feelings dissolves	Body consciousness can no longer experience the three types of feelings that accompany sense consciousness.		Vajrapani
			Shaptavajra
			Aparajita
ear sense dissolves	You can no longer hear external or internal sounds.		Takkiraja
basic wisdom of equality dissolves	You are no longer mindful of the feelings of pleasure, pain, or neutrality that usually accompany the sense consciousness.		
Third dissolution			
fire element dissolves	You cannot digest food and drink.	appearance of fireflies or sparks within smoke	Amitabha
aggregate of discrimination dissolves	You are not mindful of affairs of close persons.		Pandaravasini
			Akashagarbha
nose sense dissolves	You can no longer smell; your inhalation is weak and exhalation strong and lengthy.		Gandhavajra
			Hayagriva
basic wisdom of analysis dissolves	You can no longer remember the names of persons close to you.		Niladanda

Factor	External Sign	Internal Deities	Deities Dissolving
Fourth dissolution			
wind element dissolves	The ten winds move to heart; inhalation and exhalation ceases.	appearance of a butter lamp sputtering out	Amoghasiddhi
aggregate of compositional factors dissolves	You cannot perform physical actions.		Tara
			Lokeshvara
			Rasavajra
tongue sense dissolves	The tongue becomes thick, short; the root of tongue becomes blue; and you cannot experience smoothness or roughness, nor can you experience tastes and tangible objects.		Sarvanivarana-vishkambhini
			Sparshavajra
			Samantabhadra
			Vighnantaka
basic wisdom of achieving activities dissolves	You are no longer mindful of external worldly activities, purposes, and so forth.		Mahabala
Fifth dissolution			
eighty conceptions and basic wisdom of the dharmadhatu dissolve	The winds to the right and left channels above heart enter channel at the top of the head.	at first, flickering butter lamp, then clear vacuity filled with white appearance	Ushinisha-chakravartin
Sixth dissolution			
mind of white appearance dissolves	The winds in the right and left channels below heart enter central channel at base of spine.	clear vacuity filled with red increase	Sumbharaja
Seventh dissolution			
mind of red increase dissolves	The upper and lower winds gather at heart; then winds enter drop at heart.	at first, vacuity filled with thick darkness; then, as if swooning unconsciously	Manjushri
Eighth dissolution			
mind of black near-attainment dissolves	All winds dissolve into the very subtle life force in the indestructible drop at the heart.	the mind of the clear light of death	Guhyasamaja

and the *result* of the path is attaining the dharmakaya. As with death, we will see that the intermediate state and rebirth also have these three aspects: the starting point of the process, the process itself, and the result of that process.

In the completion stage when we reach the practice called *mental isolation*, we will go beyond imagination and actually experience the dissolutions that lead to the clear-light mind. During the generation stage, it is very important to make them feel as real as possible in our imagining, to try and see the signs of dissolution as clearly as possible. This will prepare us for when we actually experience the clear-light mind, either during the completion stage or when we die, helping our virtuous mind manifest at that crucial juncture. This meditation does not just allow us to have a better death; it is the essence of the spiritual path itself.

During the dissolutions in the completion stage, there occurs what are called the *four empties*—the empty, very empty, great empty, and all empty. These four empties are associated in ordinary death with the last four stages of the dissolution—the white appearance, red increase, black near-attainment, and clear light, first as simulated clear light and then as actual clear light. The term *simulated clear light* refers to the realization of emptiness that still has a trace of conceptuality in it, and *actual clear light* refers to the direct realization of emptiness without any conceptuality. We will revisit these terms later on. What is important to recognize here is that imagining these four empties in the generation stage will leave a strong imprint on our mind, so that when we reach the practice of mental isolation in the completion stage, we will actually be able to experience them.

In the ordinary death process, after the clear light occurs, the intermediate state happens. But in the completion stage during mental isolation, after the last of the four empties occurs at the time of the clear light, we will be able to arise into the illusory body. If that happens, we will attain full enlightenment in this very lifetime. Taking death as dharmakaya into the path is thus an important meditation because it creates the propensity to achieve the actual dharmakaya.

The Yoga of Taking the Intermediate State as the Sambhogakaya into the Path

As the consciousness moves from the ordinary clear light of the eighth dissolution into the bardo, in our meditation we move from the dharmakaya into the sambhogakaya, a buddha's enjoyment body. This is the first of the two form bodies of a buddha, the one that is able to be seen only by realized bodhisattvas.

The yoga of taking the intermediate state as the sambhogakaya into the path has five steps in the generation stage. First we meditate on emptiness and clear light and their indivisible nature, which is the dharmakaya, or truth body. This is known as the *clarification through suchness*. Then we visualize three letters—*om, ah,* and *hum*—and the sun disc, moon disc, and lotus merging into a single moon disc. This is called the *clarification through the moon*. Next we visualize the three letters on top of the moon disc, with *om* and *ah* dissolving into the *hum*. This step is known as the *clarification through the seed syllables*. After that, we visualize the five-spoked white vajra with the three letters at its hub, which is called the *clarification through the hand implements*. In the final stage, known as the *clarification through the emergence into full form*, we visualize the white primordial buddha.

THE BASE, PATH, AND RESULT IN THE BARDO PRACTICE

Each of these five clarifications in the yoga of taking the intermediate state as the sambhogakaya into the path has three levels:

+ the base level, comparable to the ordinary bardo state
+ the path level, comparable to completion-stage experiences
+ the result level, comparable to gaining full enlightenment

With the clarification through suchness, at the *base level*, the sun, moon, and lotus represent the three appearances that occur when the person comes out of the clear light of death and moves toward the bardo, starting with black near-attainment, then red increase, and finally white appearance. The three letters that transform into the sun, moon, and lotus represent the winds that carry the mind of the three appearances.

At the *path level* it is no longer imagination; these appearances actually occur. Here the sun, moon, and lotus represent white appearance, red increase, and black near-attainment, which precede the dawning of the simulated clear light and actual clear light at the completion-stage practice of mental isolation.

At the *result level*, they represent the white appearance, red increase, and black near-attainment that occur just before the attainment of the dharmakaya—that is, just before the attainment of enlightenment.

In the meditation on the clarification through the moon, the *om*, *ah*, and *hum* and the sun, moon, and lotus merge to become a single moon. We visualize that light rays are emitted from the moon disc and reach all the objects of the universe, which then dissolve back into the moon disc. This represents the fact that the entire universe and all its sentient beings have originated from the subtle consciousness and subtle wind. Dissolving everything into the moon disc signifies that the root of all phenomena is the very subtle consciousness and subtle wind.

At the *base level*, this merging signifies that the consciousness and the wind are united in one nature when we move into the intermediate state. At the *path level*, it represents the three appearances that occur at the level of mental isolation moving into the simulated clear light and actual clear light. At the *result level*, it represents the wisdom mind, or dharmakaya.

With the clarification through the seed syllables, we visualize a white *om*, red *ah*, and blue *hum* above the moon disc. They come after the previous appearance and merging of the *om*, *ah*, and *hum* and sun, moon, and lotus. As the three letters arise from the single moon, they appear "like water bubbles bursting from water," as the Guhyasamaja sadhana says. At the *base level* they represent the speech of a bardo being; on the *path level* they represent the speech of the illusory-body being; on the *result level* they represent the exalted speech of the sambhogakaya buddha.

From the moon disc and three letters, light rays are emitted toward an infinite mass of buddhas of the five families and their retinues, which then dissolve back into the moon disc. This represents the activities of the bardo being as well as the enlightened activities of the sambhogakaya.

The next meditation is the clarification through the hand implements. Here the five Dhyani Buddhas have completely dissolved into a white five-spoked vajra. At the *base level* the vajra represents the mind of the bardo being. At the *path level* it represents the mind of the illusory-body being. At the *result level* it represents the mind of the sambhogakaya buddha.

At death, the very subtle consciousness leaves the body, and the being takes the intermediate-state body. Thus, the bardo being at the ordinary level originates from the subtle mind and subtle wind, which come from the clear light. That clear light of death carries all the karmic imprints into the next life, and that includes the fundamental purity of the mind and the five primordial or basic wisdoms—of equality, analysis, and so forth.

In the visualizations we do in Vajrayana, the five spokes of the vajra represent the five primordial wisdoms. At the hub of the vajra, we visualize the three letters *om*, *ah*, and *hum*, which represent the sambhogakaya's body, speech, and mind. Quite often in Vajrayana the enlightened form is called the *union of mind and body*. Here it very much refers to the union of clear light and illusory body.

In the last meditation, on the clarification through the emergence into full form, the vajra and letters completely transform into ourselves as the white primordial buddha, which for the Guhyasamaja practice is Akshobhya sitting on the moon disc at the center of the mandala palace. At the *base level* this represents the completely formed bardo being, at the *path level* it represents the pure and impure illusory bodies, and at the *result level* it represents the sambhogakaya itself.

The Yoga of Taking Rebirth as Nirmanakaya into the Path

The visualizations involved in the yoga of taking rebirth as nirmanakaya into the path mimic the various things happen in our ordinary birth: the conception, the gestation, the actual birth, and so forth. As with ordinary birth, the start is sexual union. The long Guhyasamaja sadhana says:

> From their natural abode the male and female tathagatas embrace in union, creating streams of bodhichitta that suffuse all the realms of space with hosts of Akshobhyas in order to tame all beings.

In the visualization, just under the roof of the mandala palace is a circular beam. Under this beam, above our heads, we visualize Akshobhya in union with his consort, who is indivisible in nature with the body, speech, and mind of all the buddhas, who have all emanated from their natural abodes. This meditation corresponds to the stage in ordinary birth where the mother and father engage in sexual intercourse.

From the place where Akshobhya and his consort meet, countless streams of bodhichitta drops—vital substances that permeate the body—are released, which radiate out to the entire universe and transform into billions of Akshobhyas, one for every sentient being. (We will look at what drops are in the next chapter.) This corresponds to the ordinary birth stage where the mother's and father's 72,000 channels are filled with the white and red substances during sexual intercourse.

Then the sadhana continues:

They bless all beings to experience uncontaminated physical and mental bliss.

Next we visualize that all the Akshobhyas bless all sentient beings. Through this action, all sentient beings who are not on the spiritual path are drawn into it, those who are on the path attain liberation, and those who have already attained liberation go on to attain full enlightenment. "Blessing" all beings can also be thought of as Akshobhya leading all sentient beings to the state of the union of bliss and emptiness. This corresponds to the great pleasure the father and mother experience in the ordinary birth process due to their channels being filled with the white and red substances.

The sadhana continues with the generation of the nirmanakaya Vajradhara:

Then the Akshobhyas merge together into a single blue Akshobhya in the mandala palace.

All those emanated Akshobhyas, who are the resultant state of all the sentient beings who have become enlightened, merge into one Akshobhya. Again we visualize this Akshobhya under the circular beam of the mandala palace above our head, this time without a consort. We continue to visualize ourselves in the form of the primordial buddha at the center of the mandala seated on a cushion. Then we, the primordial buddha, lift up into the space where Akshobhya was sitting just below the beam, and Akshobhya moves down to the cushion where the primordial buddha was sitting. Next the primordial buddha slowly moves down and enters into Akshobhya's crown. This visualization corresponds to the ordinary birth stage where the bardo being's consciousness enters the crown or mouth of the father while the father and mother are engaging in sexual intercourse and emerges through the sex organ into the mother's womb. Then the white and red drops meet, and the being begins to develop into its full form.

In the sadhana we, as Akshobhya, are now called the nirmanakaya Vajradhara. This emanation of Akshobhya is blue with three faces—blue, white, and red—and six arms; holding the vajra, wheel, and lotus in the right hands, and bell, jewel, and sword in the left; and adorned with precious jewels and various robes of silk. This corresponds to the stage of the actual birth when the fetus develops.

In the meditation, in a detailed section called the *body mandala*, we visualize that the five aggregates of ourselves as three-faced, six-armed Akshobhya transform into the five Dhyani Buddhas, and the four ordinary elements of earth, fire, wind, and air transform into the four consorts or female deities. We then visualize the other attributes of our body being transformed: our eye organs transform into bodhisattvas, the five domains of sense consciousness transform into the five vajra *dakinis*, and our joints and limbs become wrathful deities. A dakini (Tib. *khandroma*) is a female being who helps arouse blissful energy in a very advanced tantric practitioner, and these five vajra dakinis are the dakinis specific to this practice.[32]

At the *base level* this represents our ordinary birth. At the *path level* it represents the creation of the gross nirmanakaya through the purification done in the completion stage. At the *result level* it represents our ability to emanate countless nirmanakayas according to the sentient beings' mental dispositions.

After this, in the sadhana, comes blessing the body, speech, and mind. Blessing the body in the practice corresponds at the ordinary level to the body in the womb being fully formed. Blessing the speech corresponds to the organs of speech, such as the tongue, being complete. Blessing the mind corresponds to the complete formation of the sense consciousnesses when the person is born.

We now visualize the three beings, or *sattvas*: the commitment being (the main deity), the wisdom being (a tiny deity at the main deity's heart), and the concentration being (a seed syllable at the wisdom being's heart). Visualizing the commitment being corresponds to the baby, newly emerged with faculties complete. Although body, speech, and mind are all complete by this stage, this consecration allows us to feel that our own body, speech, and mind are indeed divine. Visualizing the wisdom being corresponds to our subtle body, and the concentration being corresponds to our subtle mind.

After that comes the meditation called *sealing with the Lord of the Family*. The Lord of the Family is generated, the male and female deities enter into union, and we are initiated with streams of nectar flowing from this union. We visualize ourselves as Vajradhara, and at our crown we visualize a white Vajrasattva, who is the nature of our guru. He or she holds a vajra and bell and embraces the consort Vajradhatvishvari, or Queen of the Vajra Realm, who is his or her own resonance. We visualize that we are empowered by the streams of nectar that flow from the union of male and female deities, purifying all our negativities. This meditation corresponds to the time the newborn child is seen by others—in other words, when the child is the object of the eye consciousness of others.

By this stage, we have fully visualized ourselves as Guhyasamaja, the central deity of this tantra. And we do not just have a clear and vivid visualization, but we hold the divine identity of Guhyasamaja in full form as a nirmanakaya aspect.[33] Holding that clear vision of Guhyasamaja and holding the strong divine identity of ourselves as Guhyasamaja is the key factor for the success of this stage of the practice.

7 The Nature of the Body and Mind

Coarse, Subtle, and Very Subtle Body and Mind

BY THE TIME we reach the final level of the generation stage, we have achieved a very strong understanding and experience of the subtle yogas. We are able to hold a clear appearance of the entire mandala inside a tiny space, such as a point of light at the secret place at the base of the spine. And we can vividly visualize the death process up to and including the clear light, along with the intermediate state and the birth process, where that process is reversed. Now are we ready to move to the next stage of the practice, the completion stage.

The practices and realizations that make up the final part of the generation stage are very similar to the opening practices of the completion stage. But whereas in the generation stage the entire practice is done from beginning to end each time, in the completion stage each part of the practice is done individually. In other words, we should move on to the next section only after a practice has been done again and again and its appropriate realization has been achieved. This is because the practices are no longer just imagination; here they are real. We now actually arise in the body and mind that before we only visualized. Each practice builds upon the one that came before it, so without gaining experience in the first step, it is pointless to move on to the second.

Because in the completion stage we actually work with our subtle mind and body—training ourselves to move the mind into the central channel—it is crucial that we have a clear understanding of the different levels of subtlety of both the body and the mind, particularly the channels, chakras, winds, and drops.

From a Vajrayana perspective, there are said to be three types of bodies: the coarse body, the subtle body, and the very subtle body. The *coarse body* is what we normally think of when we hear the word "body": we can touch and see it; we feed it and clothe it; and it consists of flesh, bone, and blood. The *subtle body* is the network of channels, the winds or energies, and the subtle drops. The *very subtle body* is made up of the particular winds that act as a vehicle for the mind that experiences the four empties and carries the clear light. It is sometimes known as the *very subtle fundamental wind*.

This very subtle fundamental wind is sometimes called the *permanent body*. It is not that it does not rely on causes and conditions—it is impermanent in the normal way we use this term. Rather it is "permanent" in the sense that it passes from life to life and will remain even after we have attained buddhahood.

These three bodies are very important in Vajrayana, particularly in highest yoga tantra, and the more advanced we become, the more we need to understand them. We need gross substances such as blood, bone, and flesh to do highest yoga tantra practices, but we also need to understand how that coarse body coexists with the subtle and very subtle bodies in order to utilize these bodies in our practice.

Similarly, the mind, like the body, is also divided into three categories: coarse, subtle, and very subtle.

The *coarse mind* refers to our normal, everyday minds: our sensory consciousnesses, feelings, and conceptual thoughts. Among these minds there are degrees of coarseness—some are very gross and some are not—but compared with the next two types of minds, they are all coarse.

The *subtle mind* refers to the eighty conceptual thoughts that cease to function during the sixth, seventh, and eighth cycles of dissolution at death. Their dissolution gives rise to the white, red, and black appearances that we have at the time of death.

The *very subtle mind* is the clear-light mind. This only arises in a normal person at the last moment of death, or at other rare moments, such as during a sneeze or an orgasm, when it is too brief and subtle to be apprehended. For the meditator, however, it is possible to use meditation to access the clear-light mind by moving all the winds into the central channel and the heart chakra.

Channels, Chakras, Winds, and Drops

CHANNELS

In the Vajrayana system there are said to be 72,000 channels (Skt. *nadi*; Tib. *tsa*) in our subtle body. These channels make up our psychic nervous system and run parallel with our physical nervous system. This intricate network of energy lines runs throughout our entire body, branching out again and again from the chakras, or centers of energy, that are situated along the main three channels.

Each tantra interprets the three main channels somewhat differently. Some explain the nature of the channels according to their actual existence, while others focus on how they are visualized during meditations, where their colors and shapes can differ. The description here generally follows the Guhyasamaja system. Although these descriptions may seem very physical, that does not mean that the channels are material things that we can see and touch, flesh-and-blood things like veins or muscles.

In our ordinary daily lives, all of our various consciousnesses occur due to the winds flowing in the two side channels. If we can empty them, those ordinary consciousnesses—sensory consciousnesses and conceptual elaboration—will stop. This is one of the main aims of the completion stage.

The channels that branch directly from the chakras are the ones that we use in our visualizations. They are:

+ the thirty-two starting from the crown chakra
+ the sixteen starting from the throat chakra
+ the eight starting from the heart chakra
+ the sixty-four starting from the navel chakra
+ the thirty-two starting from the secret-place chakra

It is mainly through these channels that the winds and the red and white drops travel.

However, our main focus should be on the central, left, and right channels. Of those, the central channel (Skt. *avadhuti*) is the most important, because great bliss is generated when the winds are moved into it, and within the central channel, the most important area is the heart chakra at the center of the chest. During our ordinary death and birth, it is at the hub of the heart chakra that our ordinary consciousness departs when we die and enters when we take a new birth. When we are on the completion-stage meditation of the simulated and actual clear light, we start at the center of the heart chakra. Thus it is important to focus on the central channel, in order to gain the clearest possible visualization of the heart chakra within it.

Ordinarily while we are alive the central channel does not really function because the right and left channels form knots at the various chakras, effectively squashing it. Very often in meditation the visualizations we do will be slightly different, so we could easily become confused unless we know how the channels actually exist.

The central channel starts at a point between the eyebrows, rises to below the crown, then curves until it follows the spine downward, a little way in front of the spine. It ends at the tip of the sexual organ. The central channel is generally said to be red inside and white outside, although this varies slightly depending on which commentary we read—some masters say that it is reddish or simply red and white, and some say it has no distinctive color at all. The central channel has four attributes: it is very straight from the crown to the navel chakra, like a trunk; its inside is very oily and red in color, like pure blood; it is clear and transparent; and it is very soft and flexible, like a plant that has just sprouted.

The winds flow through the central channel naturally at the time of death, but the goal of the completion stage is to move the mind carried by the winds into the central channel through meditation while we are still alive. Thus the central channel is also known as the *mind channel*. Another name for it is the *two abandonments*, because when the winds enter it, they dissolve, and the two obscurations are thereby abandoned. In this context, the obscuration to knowledge or omniscience is called the *obscuration to the achievement of clear light*.

The right channel (Skt. *rasana*), which is red, is called the *speech channel* because red drops, the essence of speech, flow through it. Another name for it is the *channel of the subjective holder*, because the main function of the winds that flow through it in our everyday lives is to make our consciousness move toward an object. It is also called the *sun channel*. Because this everyday consciousness is a conceptual mind, it creates a degree of subjectivity that hinders us from perceiving the object directly without any conceptual overlay.

The left channel (Skt. *lalana*), which is white, is called the *body channel* because white drops, the essence of the body, flow through it. Its other names are the *moon channel* and the *channel of the held object*, the latter because one of the main functions of the winds that flow in it is to hold an object, such as form or sound.

The left and right channels start at the nostrils and then rise up, as the central channel does, to just below the crown before coming down either side of the central channel, ending like the central channel at the tip of the sex organ. In meditations, we are often asked to visualize all three channels coming together four finger-widths below the navel.

It is important to remember that although the right and left channels run parallel to the central channel, they are not completely straight. They twist at the chakras due to the conceptual thoughts traveling through them. These twists are usually called *knots*, but they are more like kinks or twists that move to the left, curve around, and then loop back to the right again, or vice versa.

During a normal person's life these knots will always be there, restricting the central channel and stopping any winds from moving within it. The Tibetan name for this state, *long-nga*, means "blind."[34] For an ordinary person it is only at the very last stage of the death process that the side channels loosen and the winds inside them flow into the central channel, allowing the clear light to become active. The goal of the completion stage is to activate this process through meditation.

We can do a practice called *cleansing the channels* (Tib. *tsalam shangpa*) that helps to activate the central channel and protects our mind from possible harm during the practice. This practice starts with the nine-round breathing meditation, but here we actually manipulate the winds, making it a very powerful practice.

We visualize the three main channels, with the left and right channels entering the central channel four finger-widths below the navel rather than where they actually do. As we do the nine-round breathing meditation, we actually feel each channel being cleansed, and because we are doing a completion-stage meditation, this is no longer imagination; we actually do this.

Although cleansing the channels is not a difficult practice, I must give a big warning here that applies to this practice and all the practices that follow it. If you try to do this without proper preparation—which means a thorough grounding in the graduated path—and without a stable deity practice, you will lose your mind. I mean that quite literally. You really need to know what you are doing; otherwise all sorts of things can start to happen. If the energies move into a wrong area, moving them back again is incredibly difficult. There are many meditators who have gone completely crazy because they have not followed the practices correctly or tried to take shortcuts.

CHAKRAS

At the various places where the right and left channels twist around the central channel, there are concentrations of energy where lines of energy radiate out, multiplying and spreading throughout our body. These places are sometimes called *channel wheels*, but they are most commonly known by their Sanskrit name, *chakra* (Tib. *tsakhor*). The lines of energy are called *spokes* or sometimes *petals*, but neither name is a good description of their shape. They most closely resemble a tree, where a main branch splits into two smaller branches that each split into smaller branches and so forth. Each branch looks like a soft plastic straw that has been blocked at one end and blown through until it bulges slightly.

The number of chakras we have in our body depends on the number of knots we have in the right and left channel. The number also varies depending on the meditation; some meditations utilize five chakras, some utilize six, and some even have ten. However in general it is said that there are five larger chakras and three smaller ones.

The five main chakras are located at the crown, the throat, the heart, the navel, and the secret place (the lower end of the spine). The three smaller chakras are a six-spoked chakra between the eyebrows, a three-spoked chakra between the throat and heart, and an eight-spoked chakra in the middle of the sex organ. Here we will focus on the five main chakras.

The chakras are either triangular or round. The triangle is always backward-facing with the apex at the back and the flat base facing the front. It is not as exact as a mathematical triangle with perfectly straight lines. And neither triangular nor round chakras are completely flat; they bend either slightly downward or slightly upward. Thus the crown chakra is a triangle whose corners droop slightly downward, the throat chakra is a disc that is slightly raised at the edges, and so forth. Chakras are either red or white, although again this can vary depending on the practice.

The crown chakra is called the *chakra of great bliss* because the white drop that helps to increase great bliss exists mainly in the crown chakra. This chakra is white, triangular, and faces downward. There are thirty-two spokes at the crown chakra. Here, the right and left channels twist around the central channel, forming a knot or coil between the brain and the scalp. The right channel twists to the left around the central channel, and the left channel twists around it to the right before they both realign and move down, creating four twists in all. It is here that the spokes begin. The four spokes each divide in half, becoming eight; the eight then divide to become sixteen; and those divide again to become thirty-two.

The throat chakra is called the *enjoyment chakra* because it is through our throat that food and drink pass, which are things we enjoy. Here we are not referring to normal food and drink but the offerings of food and drink we make during our deity practice. The throat chakra is red, round, and faces upward. This chakra is located between the neck bone and the voice box. It divides in half in the same way as the crown chakra, with the four spokes caused by the knots in the side channels becoming eight and then sixteen.

The heart chakra is called the *phenomena chakra* because it is the abode of the indestructible drop (the very subtle body) and clear light (the very subtle mind), which are the root of all external and internal phenomena. This chakra is white, round, and faces downward. The heart chakra is not located where our physical heart is but in the exact middle of our chest. Some texts say that there is one knot at the heart; others that there are three. In both cases it divides once to become eight spokes.

The navel chakra is called the *emanation chakra* because during the completion-stage practice, heat emanates from this wheel. This melts the white drop at our crown and causes it to start to flow down, generating great bliss. This chakra is red, triangular, and faces upward. The navel chakra is not where our actual navel is but one or two finger-widths below it; its exact location can differ slightly from individual to individual. Here the number of spokes is sixty-four—four becoming eight, becoming sixteen, becoming thirty-two, becoming sixty-four.

The secret-place chakra is called the *utilizing great bliss chakra*. This is because in the completion-stage meditation when the four empties and four joys are experienced, there is a particular meditation called the *innate great bliss meditation* that is practiced in forward and reverse order at the secret place. The secret place chakra is red, round, and faces downward. It has thirty-two spokes, divided in the same way as the crown.

To summarize, table 4 outlines the chakras as described in the Guhyasamaja system.

LOOSENING THE KNOTS

As we have seen, the completion stage is to be done step by step. Only when we have completely mastered the meditation on cleansing the

TABLE 4. THE CHAKRAS

CHAKRA	NAME	SHAPE	DIRECTION	NUMBER	COLOR
crown	great bliss	triangular	down	32	white
throat	enjoyment	round	up	16	red
heart	phenomena	round	down	8	white
navel	emanation	triangular	up	64	red
secret place	utilizing great bliss	round	down	32	red

channels described above should we go on to this practice of loosen-ing the knots.

The first part of the practice is to visualize the deity. Whatever deity we are practicing, we visualize ourselves as that deity with one face and two arms and a body that is completely transparent, like a resin statue that we can see right through. Every detail is clear—the nails, each strand of hair, everything—and they are all completely transparent. In Tibetan this is called *tongra gompa*, which literally means "medi-tating on the hollow body."

After strongly establishing the visualization, we concentrate on visu-alizing the channels, starting with the central channel. Although in reality the side channels are active and the central channel is "blind" or inactive, we visualize them as if it were the other way around, with the side channels flat and inactive and the central channel really full.

Then we visualize the chakras. For the Guhyasamaja practice, we start at the heart because that is the most important chakra and the hardest one to loosen the knots around. At the heart chakra three knots are visualized. From the second knot the spokes of the chakra start to spread out, four and then eight, turning slightly downward as they expand. The other chakras are visualized in the same way. After that, we need to take the time to firmly establish the visualization, going up and down the central channel making sure each chakra is visualized clearly.

The next step is to prepare the path of the channels. In the second of the three knots of the heart chakra, we visualize a tiny drop with a reddish-white hue. We cultivate the thought that this drop is the essence of our root masters, the principal deities, and each of their three doors of mind, body, and speech. If this step sounds impossible, remember that by this stage we will have already attained calm abiding, so we will be used to visualizing such minute details.

Next comes a step where we visualize our mind entering into the drop and the mind and the drop becoming one. The mind enters the drop at the center of the heart chakra, and then that drop (which is one with our mind) begins to move around, starting at the front and then moving to the right and left. It looks through the channels and spokes that start from the heart chakra and sees them as hollow without any obstructions.

When our mind sees that the channel and spokes are free from any obstructions, we move to the next stage, where we look down from the heart chakra to the navel chakra and then to the secret-place chakra. After that we look upward and examine the throat chakra and the crown chakra. We are checking that the path truly is hollow and free from obstructions. For me, it feels like we have a really powerful flashlight and we are looking up this hollow transparent tube, able to see everything.

At the next stage of the meditation we ride up the central channel to the center of the throat chakra. As with the heart chakra, we start by making a full circle around it, examining the color, the way the knot is formed, the way its spokes radiate out, everything.

After that, we move to the crown chakra, circling it and coming to rest at its center. After inspecting the entire chakra, we look at how it rests at the exact top of the central channel. It bulges out, half in the central channel and half out. We are not talking about the physical body here, but if we were, the chakra would protrude slightly from the crown. It is as if we have come to the top of a high tower, where we can look out and see the entire mandala with all the attendant deities before us.

Finally we gently move down through the chakras, first from the crown chakra back through the central channel; then looking down at the throat chakra and moving toward it; then moving to the heart chakra, the navel chakra, and the secret-place chakra. By doing this, we are loosening the knots at each of the chakras. This is a very exacting meditation. If we get tired, we should stop for a while and do some prayers and dedications.

WINDS

The winds (Skt. *vayu*; Tib. *lung*) are what move through the channels; they are the energies in our body that cause all movement—external bodily movement, the internal activity of organs and muscles, the circulation of blood and air, and the movement of substances such as urine and waste. They are also the vehicles for our various consciousnesses to make contact with their respective objects. We utilize the winds in our Vajrayana practice, so it is important that we understand them.

Wind is the air we breathe but it is also these psychic energies, and on this more subtle level it relates to the idea of the "vital force" that is common to many philosophies. In Sanskrit it is called *prana*, which is a major part of Hindu yoga practices. In Chinese it is called *qi* (*chi*); manipulating it is one of the key elements of acupuncture. And in Tibetan it is called *sog*, and it is central to several Buddhist practices, including the tantra of our discussion. In tantra it is described as a combination of life and "heat" that the consciousness enters to begin a new rebirth. Unfortunately, most people in the West seem to have lost touch with this important concept.

The winds are used in the three lower levels of tantra, such as in the practice of holding the wind in a vase, but these are comparatively coarser winds, and those practices are crude compared to the ones we use in highest yoga tantra. Here the practices are much more complex than stopping the grosser winds from escaping outside in order to still our conceptual thoughts. In highest yoga tantra we are trying to move the more subtle winds into the central channel and then dissolve them into the center of the heart chakra, where the indestructible drop and clear light are. The first stage of the completion stage, physical isolation, involves connecting with the winds. This comes before we can control them and make them enter, abide, and dissolve into the central channel. But even connecting with them is a far more advanced practice than the vase breathing we saw in the lower tantras.

The wind that suffuses our body has different functions, and so the tantric texts consider five major root winds and five secondary branch winds.[35] The major winds are:

+ life-supporting, or vital (*prana*)
+ downward-voiding (*apana*)
+ upward-moving (*udana*)
+ equally abiding (*samana*)
+ pervading (*vyana*)

When studying the major winds, for each one there are different things we should know, summarized in table 5.

Each wind is associated with a particular color and Dhyani Buddha. For example, the life-supporting wind is white and associated with Akshobhya, and the downward-voiding wind is yellow and associated with Ratnasambhava. This information becomes important later on when we do the body mandala, where each wind turns into a particular Dhyani Buddha.

Each wind is also associated with a particular element: the upward-moving wind with fire, the pervading wind with space, and so on. And

TABLE 5. THE WINDS AND THE FIVE DHYANI BUDDHAS[36]

	Life-Supporting	Downward-Voiding	Upward-Moving	Equally Abiding	Pervading
Buddha Family	Akshobhya	Ratna-sambhava	Amitabha	Amoghasiddhi	Vairochana
Color	white	yellow	red	green	pale blue
Element	water	earth	fire	wind	space
Seat	heart	navel	throat	the two lower doors: the anus and the sex organ	both the upper and lower parts of the body, mainly the 360 joints
Function	to support and maintain life	to retain and release urine, feces, semen, blood, etc.	to speak, swallow, etc.	to cause the blazing of the inner fire, digest food and drink, etc.	to enable the body to come and go; to allow movement, lifting, and placing
Direction	from both nostrils, gently downward	from both nostrils, horizontally forward heavily	from the right nostril, violently upward	from the left nostril, moving to the left and right from the edge of the nostril	this wind does not flow through the nostrils except at the time of death

although certain winds, like the pervading wind, can be situated anywhere in the body, most have a location. For instance, the life-supporting wind is at the heart, and the upward-moving wind is at throat.

The functions you can see on the chart are gross generalizations, but it is still very interesting to look at them. The function of the life-supporting or vital wind is just that: to support and maintain life.[37]

The function of the downward-voiding, or evacuating, wind is retaining and releasing urine, water, and other similar substances. The upward-moving, or ascending, wind assists speaking, swallowing, and so on. The function of the equally abiding, or metabolic, wind is to cause the inner fire to blaze as well as to digest food and so on. The pervading wind enables the body's movements.

It is very easy to think of these winds as somehow entirely different from the air we breathe; in fact they are similar. But as with all of the substances we are looking at, the distinction is one of subtlety. For instance, the air that moves through our nostrils and that which we use in vase breathing is coarse, whereas the pervading wind is much subtler.

The direction of each wind given in the chart might seem a bit strange. At present all we know is that we breathe, and our breath is not hard to follow in its course in and out of our body. Until we reach the stage in our practice where our mind is subtle enough that we can actually perceive them, we have no way of knowing the directions that the subtle winds take. When we do, we can start to manipulate them. However, whether we are aware of them or not, these winds are operating all the time. The hardest wind to dissolve—through meditation or even during the natural process of death—is the pervading wind, since it is the only wind that does not flow through the nostrils in normal life but only at the time of death.

The significance, location, and function of all five major winds are important to know for completion-stage practice, particularly when we reach the level of verbal isolation practice.

Drops

Another substance that it is important to know about is the drops (Skt. *bindu* or *tilaka*; Tib. *tig-le*).[38] Drops are substances that permeate our body, caused by the coalescing of the mind and its accompanying wind at certain areas of the body. There are grosser drops and subtler ones, with the grosser ones consisting of subtle, essential bodily fluids such as bile concentrating in different points as the winds move them about the body. The subtler ones are purely mind and its accompanying wind, and this is what we are interested in, in tantra. These subtler drops are also often called *bodhichitta drops* or even just *bodhichitta* (Tib. *jangsem*) in the tantric sadhanas.

The origin of the drops is the indestructible drop that originates from the male and female's white and red drops; thus the drops themselves are of two types, white and red.[39]

Although drops originate at the center of the heart chakra, most texts say that the white drops that evolve from the original white drop abide at the crown and the red drops that evolve from the original red drop abide at the navel. In the meditation the white drop at the crown is signified by a *hum* and the red drop at the navel by an *om*. In reality, the drops pervade our entire body; this distinction is drawn mainly to help our meditation. These drops are subtler than the ones at the crown and navel that the texts talk about.

The indestructible drop, the origin of all the drops, itself originates from the father's white drop and the mother's red one and is the basis for the physical body. We talk of the indestructible drop as one entity, but in fact it consists of two elements. Generally, when we say "indestructible drop" we mean the indestructible drop of this life, which is a very subtle material object that is destroyed at the end of our life. It is the size of a small pea, white on top and red below, almost like a small spherical container of two parts; it can be split in two at death, allowing the eternal indestructible drop, the very subtle wind and mind, to be released.[40]

The very subtle consciousness and its wind that leave the body at death is the eternal indestructible drop. It carries through the bardo, and it enters the womb of the mother at conception. It is called "eternal" because of the continuation that is always there, not because it is unchanging. The very subtle fundamental wind the consciousness rides on is the permanent body we looked at above.

In a sense, the indestructible drop is the container, and the mind and wind inside are the contents. Mind and wind depend on each other—without mind there can be no wind, and without wind there can be no mind—and it is the container of the indestructible drop that holds them together.

THE ENLIGHTENMENT PROCESS

Not until we can fully appreciate how these subtle aspects of our mind and body—the channels, chakras, winds, and drops—operate will we be able to start working with them and, as we progress in our completion-stage practice, manipulating them in a way that profoundly affects our life. Vajrayana is so powerful, and yet it is so subtle.

Mind and body coexist. When we look at the subtle body and the very subtle body, we see that coarse minds such as anger and attachment and coarse winds coexist; that the subtle minds such as the eighty conceptual thoughts coexist with, and are carried on, the subtle winds; and that the very subtle minds and winds operate together. In other words, the winds and the minds carried on those winds are interdependent.

The very subtle wind (the very subtle body) is the energy that carries the clear light (the very subtle mind); the two are inseparable. In our normal life, this inseparable very subtle mind and wind are the basis of samsara—they lead us into the next life and the next and the next. But as a practitioner of highest yoga tantra, we can use them to attain liberation and enlightenment. Thus they are sometimes called the "basis of samsara and liberation." In the enlightenment process, the subtlest wind is the substantial cause for the rupakaya, or form body, and the subtlest mind is the substantial cause for the dharmakaya. The inseparability of these two is the substantial cause for the union of the two bodies of a buddha, which is enlightenment. We cannot undertake any meditation practice where we try to manipulate these subtle elements without a thorough understanding of the coarse, subtle, and very subtle levels of body and mind that we all have.

Emptiness and Bliss

EMPTINESS, BLISS, AND THE MEANING OF *Evam*

In the completion stage, we have moved from imagining manipulating our winds to actually being able to do it. Once again, the final goal is to move the winds into the central channel and then into the center of the heart chakra and dissolve them into the indestructible drop there. This is the actual mechanics of becoming enlightened. The channels, chakras, winds, and drops are the tools we use in implementing that enlightenment process.

When we reach the final stage, we experience what is called the union of emptiness and great bliss. This is symbolized by the two-syllable word *evam*. It is a term that often comes into highest yoga tantra sadhanas and prayers and is a kind of shorthand that sums up the whole process that leads to the final union. This word not only encompasses the whole meaning of the completion-stage practice, but it is in some sense the very essence of the body of highest yoga tantra teachings.

The word is made up of two syllables, *e* and *vam*, and the *vam* itself consists of two sounds, the letter *wa* (for the Sanskrit *va*) and the *m*, a nasal stop that is notated by the circle called an *anusvara* above the letter.

Evam has three levels: base, path, and result. At the *base level*, the *e* represents the crown and navel chakras, which are triangular; the *wa* represents the heart and throat chakras, which are round; and the *m* represents focusing on these chakras using the right methods. Great bliss is generated when the melting bodhichitta is drawn down from the crown and up from the secret place; that union is also represented by the *m*. The inseparable nature of great bliss and emptiness is *evam*.

At the *path level*, the syllable *e* represents the wisdom realizing emptiness during the path; the *wa* represents experiencing great bliss during the path; and the *m* represents the inseparable nature of these two
realizations. Thus at the path level *evam* represents the inseparable
nature of the wisdom realizing emptiness and the experience of great
bliss.

With the *evam* that corresponds to the *result level*, the *e* refers to the
direct realization of emptiness by the wisdom of a buddha; the *wa* symbolizes the great bliss of the wisdom of a buddha; and the inseparability of great bliss and the realization of emptiness in the wisdom of a
buddha is symbolized by the *m*.

At the result level *evam* also represents the union of the two truths—
ultimate truth and conventional truth. Here, the first syllable *e* represents the inseparable nature of a buddha's wisdom and great bliss. The
wa, represents a buddha's form body, and the anusvara, the *m*, represents the unitary nature of body and mind. In other words, a buddha's
realization of emptiness and experience of great bliss and a buddha's
body are a single entity. So *evam* symbolizes these two truths, where
ultimate truth refers to the inseparable nature of a buddha realizing
emptiness and experiencing great bliss, and the conventional truth is
a buddha's form body.

The Union of Emptiness and Great Bliss

Each of the four Buddhist philosophical schools presents emptiness
differently.[41] There is the emptiness or selflessness asserted by the
schools below Svatantrika-Madhyamaka, where the Hinayana
schools—Vaibhashika and Sautrantika—assert emptiness is being
empty of substantial existence and the Chittamatra school explains
emptiness as the absence of duality of appearance of subject and object.
The Svatantrika-Madhyamaka school explains it as being empty of

existing from its own side without depending on the mind. Finally, there is the emptiness asserted in Prasangika-Madhyamaka, which is being empty of existing inherently.

There are no teachings in Vajrayana on the union of great bliss with the first emptiness, the emptiness of substantial existence. There are teachings about the union of great bliss with the emptiness asserted by the Chittamatra and Svatantrika-Madhyamaka schools. But in the context of highest yoga tantra practice—particularly when we are talking about the practice of the jewel-like practitioner, the highest level of meditator—the union of emptiness and great bliss refers specifically to the definition of emptiness asserted by Prasangika-Madhyamaka.

The other side of the union, bliss, also has different levels. We experience one kind of bliss when we gain actual calm abiding. We experience the second level, known as *uncontaminated bliss*, when we realize emptiness directly. In the three lower classes of Vajrayana, a meditator who successfully does the vase-breathing meditation based on deity yoga experiences another level of bliss. Yet another type of bliss is experienced during consort practice, when the practitioner mentally or actually embraces the consort.

There is a further level of bliss that occurs as the meditator advances in the completion stage, when he or she is able to manipulate the winds but before they enter and dissolve in the central channel. At some stage of the meditation, the drop that resides at the crown chakra is loosened and starts to descend, but because the knots at the side channels still block the central channel, it is not able to travel there. Even so, that loosening of the drop brings a profound sense of bliss.

The fifth and final level of bliss is the great bliss experienced in the completion stage, when the winds actually enter, abide, and dissolve into the central channel. That bliss is called *innate great bliss*. This is the bliss of the union of emptiness and great bliss in highest yoga tantra.

Even though there are these different types of emptiness and different types of bliss, whenever we refer to the union of emptiness and great bliss in highest yoga tantra, we are always talking about the innate great bliss generated during the completion stage and the Prasangika definition of emptiness. In the indivisible union between wisdom realizing emptiness and the profound experience of great bliss, wisdom and bliss are experienced within a single consciousness. This is a practice unique to highest yoga tantra.

What comes first, wisdom realizing emptiness or the experience of great bliss? There are two possibilities. If we have gained a realization of emptiness based on the teachings of the Chittamatra or Svatantrika schools, that understanding can ignite the inner heat (Skt. *chandali*; Tib. *tumo*), allowing the winds to enter, abide, and dissolve into the central channel. From that experience of great bliss we will slowly and naturally move to the highest understanding of emptiness asserted by the Prasangika school.

For most highest yoga tantra practitioners, however, the sequence works the other way around. We first gain the highest wisdom realizing emptiness of inherent existence and then experience of great bliss.

8 THE SIX LEVELS OF THE COMPLETION STAGE

IN THE PREVIOUS CHAPTER we looked in some detail at the subtle physiology and the way it relates to the mind. In this chapter we are going to look at the actual practices of the completion stage. Here again we will use Guhyasamaja tantra as a model. Most other highest yoga tantra completion-stage sadhanas have a similar outline.[42] Everything the Buddha taught in his more than forty years of teaching was to lead the practitioner to enlightenment, and according to the teachings on highest yoga tantra, enlightenment can only come from the most subtle mind entering and dissolving in the center of the heart chakra and the dharmakaya being achieved.[43] So, in some ways, every aspect of the Buddhist path leads to this point, where the practitioner works through the six levels of the completion stage of highest yoga tantra to finally attain enlightenment.

The completion-stage practices are a gradual refining of the meditations on the winds, where we are moving the winds with more and more skill, first into the central channel, then the heart chakra, and finally the indestructible drop. This process, which happens during ordinary death before the bardo commences and is mimicked in the generation stage, is now actually experienced through meditation.

In the completion stage we have gone beyond imagination and are trying to actually experience the death process, particularly the last four stages of the dissolution, the four empties, which occur during the minds of white appearance, red increase, black near-attainment, and clear light. Here, the four empties are actually experienced by the power of the meditation.

At the same time that we experience the four empties, the different levels of bliss are experienced. During the last part of the generation stage, some practitioners can generate the deity through the mind realizing emptiness and experience bliss, but this is not considered a completion-stage practice because the winds still have not entered and dissolved into the central channel. Only in the completion stage do we experience great bliss that is generated into the deity. In fact that is the very definition of the completion stage:

> [The completion stage is] a yoga in the mindstream of a trainee that has arisen from the winds entering, abiding, and dissolving in the central channel by the power of meditation.[44]

As we have seen, we can cause the winds to naturally enter, abide, and dissolve into the central channel through the meditations of cleansing the channels and loosening the knots.

There will be various deities mentioned in the discussion below, and it might seem a little bewildering to somebody not actually practicing Guhyasamaja. During the different stages the practitioner generates him- or herself as Guhyasamaja with one face and two arms or as Akshobhya or Vajradhara with three faces and six arms. Although rarely explicitly stated, the deity will usually be in union with a consort. This will be a "wisdom seal" or visualized consort, or an "action seal" or actual consort, depending on the level of attainment of the practitioner. (We will look at this below.) All these deities, alone and with consort, are however all aspects of the enlightened mind, and represent the various stages of the practice of taking death, intermediate state, and rebirth as the three kayas into the path, as well as the other stages of subtlety reached in the different levels of the completion stage. In general, the elaborate visualizations of the generation stage, designed to increase the ability of the mind to hold ever-smaller and more detailed images, are left behind as the practitioner does not just visualize him- or herself as a deity but actually arises as a deity.

There are different ways of counting the stages of the completion stage according to the Guhyasamaja practice. Some texts divide the completion stage into five levels, with physical and verbal isolation counted as one, but I will divide the practice into six, following the Guhyasamaja root tantra and the sixth chapter of Chandrakirti's commentary, the *Bright Lamp* (*Pradipodyotana*), the main commentary on the Guhyasamaja tantra in the Arya tradition of Nagarjuna's *Five Stages* (*Panchakrama*).[45]

The six levels of the completion stage are:

+ physical isolation
+ verbal isolation
+ mental isolation
+ illusory body
+ actual clear light
+ union

As our mind becomes more profound and subtle in meditation, we slowly move through these six stages. There is no shortcut. Each stage brings us closer to the final goal of the union of clear light and illusory body.

Physical Isolation

As we have seen, the distinction between the last part of the generation stage and the first part of the completion stage is not always clear. There are some differences in the assertions of the commentaries, where some say that the physical-isolation practice falls within the subtle yoga of the generation stage and others put it entirely in the completion stage. Some practitioners, on the other hand, assert that within the several different stages of the realizations that count as physical-isolation practices, some belong to the generation stage and some to the completion stage. This is the model I will follow.

There are three physical-isolation practices. Two of them are generation-stage practices that correspond to the practitioner's level of capability. During the first level we can generate the deities purely from the realization of emptiness; they are not generated by the meditation on bliss at all. During the second level we generate into the deity through the experience of bliss realizing emptiness. This bliss, however, is not due to the winds entering, abiding, and dissolving into the central channel but due to certain meditations.

The last physical isolation practice is the bliss realizing emptiness, generated by the winds entering, abiding, and dissolving into the central channel. The bodhichitta drop melts, and we experience great bliss. Through that great bliss we realize emptiness, and then that understanding is generated into the deity. This type of physical isolation belongs to the completion stage. The definition is thus:

> Physical isolation in the completion stage is a yoga such that, while in meditative equipoise, one meditates on the wisdom of bliss and emptiness arising from the winds dissolving in the central channel. Waking up from that in the post-meditation period, all objects that appear are sealed by bliss and emptiness and arise in the aspects of deities, such as those of the hundred families.
>
> Physical isolation is so called because it is a yoga that seals the body [the basis of isolation] composed of the aggregates, elements, sense sources, and so forth within one's continuum, by

the bliss and emptiness of the completion stage. Having isolated the body from ordinary appearances and grasping, it appears in the aspect of pure deities. In general, physical isolation contains parts of both the generation and completion stages.[46]

Think of an artist who can use the same color blue to paint picture after picture. Or think of an opera or play with a performer who can wear different masks and perform different roles. The same thing is happening here—due to the meditation on the winds entering, abiding, and dissolving into the central channel and experiencing great bliss, one single mind can manifest as many different deities.

We call these practices *physical isolation* because at this stage we are isolating the twenty-five "physical" aspects of the coarse body and mind,[47] although they are not all physical in the everyday sense of the word. These twenty-five gross phenomena are the basis of the physical isolation; they are the objects that are actually turned into the deities by the single mind experiencing great bliss while realizing emptiness, which is what the term "meditative equipoise" (Skt. *samahita*; Tib. *nyamzhag*) means here. This is not the direct realization of emptiness that transforms one into an arya being—that does not occur until the stage of clear light—but it is a close approximation. "Isolation" means our mind is isolated from any sense of ordinariness in these twenty-five physical things; they will no longer appear as ordinary but as the twenty-five deities of the body mandala.

When we meditate on physical isolation, the winds enter, abide, and dissolve into the central channel. Due to that dissolution, great bliss is experienced, and then that mind realizes emptiness. It is that mind that is generated into the deity. In the case of Guhyasamaja, there are four ways of doing this, differentiated mainly in terms of how many deities they use. Thus the names of the four practices are:

+ the ultimate physical isolation of the hundred deities
+ the ultimate physical isolation of the twenty-five deities
+ the ultimate physical isolation of the secret three families
+ the ultimate physical isolation of one great secret family

The first method is the *ultimate physical isolation of the hundred deities*. In it a hundred deities are generated from the elements of the practitioner's body. Each aggregate is generated into the five Dhyani Buddhas (which makes twenty-five deities), and then the four elements are generated into four consorts, with each consort generated for each of the five Dhyani Buddhas (making twenty). Then the six sense sources are generated into six bodhisattvas, with one set for each Dhyani Buddha (making thirty). Finally the five sense objects are generated into the five offering dakinis for each Dhyani Buddha (making twenty-five). All together this totals a hundred deities.

The second method, the *ultimate physical isolation of the twenty-five deities*, is a little less elaborate. Here consciousness and the four elements, which make the five phenomena within us, are visualized as the five Dhyani Buddhas, making twenty-five. The air element generates into Vairochana, the water element generates into Ratnasambhava, the fire element generates into Amitabha, the wind element generates into Amoghasiddhi, and the consciousness generates into Akshobhya. This is done using the same process as above: We visualize the winds entering, abiding, and dissolving into the central channel and the bodhichitta drop melting and great bliss increasing. Through the experience of bliss, the mind realizes emptiness, and from that the mind is generated into the five deities using the four elements and consciousness.

The third method, the *ultimate physical isolation of the secret three families*, uses the same process. This time the mind experiencing great bliss and realizing emptiness uses the three doors of body, speech, and mind to generate six deities. The body is generated into Ratnasambhava and Vairochana as the vajra body, the speech is generated into

Amoghasiddhi and Amitabha as the vajra speech, and the mind is generated as Vajradhara and Akshobhya as the vajra mind.

In the last method, the *ultimate physical isolation of the one great secret family*, using the same process, we visualize the three doors of body, speech, and mind transformed into the three doors of Vajradhara.

In each of these four methods the process is the same. The difference comes after the inseparability of great bliss and emptiness has been achieved, when that realization is generated into different numbers of deities. There is no need to start with the "simple" single-deity practice and then work up to the hundred. At this stage of our development, one is no more difficult to visualize than the other. The idea is to increase divine pride and concentration, and we use whatever method is most applicable.

Whichever of the four methods we use—the hundred, twenty-five, three, or one—during the meditation three aspects are experienced:

+ mental bliss
+ the bliss of pliancy
+ single-pointed meditative stabilization (*shamatha*)

These three—mental bliss, the bliss of pliancy, and single-pointed meditative stabilization—are all experienced within the single mind that is inseparable from great bliss and emptiness. That state is usually referred to as *meditative equipoise*. This is what we do in the main meditation session during the physical isolation stage.

THE ACTUAL MEDITATION OF PHYSICAL ISOLATION

The meditation on physical isolation has three divisions:

+ the meditation on a subtle drop
+ the meditation on emptiness
+ maintaining meditative equipoise on emptiness during the post-meditation session

The first division, the *meditation on a subtle drop*, is done in order to draw the winds into the central channel. Having achieved both the gross and subtle generation-stage realizations, we generate ourselves into Vajradhara and have a strong sense of divine identity as Vajradhara. This subtle-drop meditation is almost the continuation of the subtle-drop meditation in the generation-stage practice. Here the difference is that after we generate ourselves into Vajradhara by means of the winds entering, abiding, and dissolving into the central channel, we experience great bliss and through that realize emptiness.

Then, at the lower end of the central channel at the tip of the sexual organ, we visualize a tiny subtle drop. Within that we visualize the entire mandala and its deities and the representations of all kinds of objects within it. The mind and the winds work together, so when we concentrate very intensely on that point, the winds will start to be drawn into that place. Then the lower part of the central channel will open, and the winds will enter into it.

Usually when we breathe, the wind passing through the right nostril is a bit more forceful than that passing through the left. But when the winds enter the central channel, the breathing will become very balanced, with neither side more forceful than the other. The sign of the winds abiding in the central channel is that the winds that normally pass through our nostrils will stop altogether. When the winds dissolve into the central channel, the same internal signs that we saw in the death process will occur again—a mirage, black smoke, fireflies, and the other appearances.

The second division of physical isolation is the *meditation on emptiness*. When the winds enter into the central channel, the downward-voiding wind, whose seat is normally at the lower abdomen just below the navel chakra, moves upward. This uncharacteristic movement of the downward-voiding wind ignites internal heat, and due to that the subtle substances—the white and red bodhichitta drops—melt. That melting and flowing to various spots in the body brings us an intense feeling of bliss. The consciousness that experiences that blissful feeling is an incredibly powerful mind; it can be used to realize emptiness.

In Guhyasamaja, this practice of generating heat or *tumo* at the navel chakra area through the melting of the two substances is done by moving the wind into the central channel and igniting the heat. The *tumo* in other deity practices such as Chakrasamvara tantra is a different practice, not part of Guhyasamaja. We will, however, briefly look at it below.

This feeling of bliss we are talking about comes through meditation, but it can also occur for the nonpractitioner in an orgasm during sexual intercourse. In this ordinary pleasure the white bodhichitta drop melts and flows but not into the central channel and only very temporarily. The great bliss that we experience through meditation, where the central channel opens and the winds enter, abide, and dissolve into it, is much more powerful.

Through this meditation, we experience different levels of bliss, or joy. Due to the winds dissolving into the central channel, the white bodhichitta drop melts and moves down from the crown to the throat, to the heart, to the navel, and finally to the secret region. At each of these four stages, four different types of joy are experienced. They are:

+ joy, when the bodhichitta drop moves from the crown to the throat
+ supreme joy, when the bodhichitta drop moves from the throat to the heart
+ special joy, when the bodhichitta drop moves from the heart to the navel
+ innate joy, when the bodhichitta drop moves from the navel to the secret place

The four joys can be experienced not only when the white drop descends from the crown to the secret place but also when the red drop moves from the secret place upward to the crown. When the latter occurs, although the joys experienced at each of the four places on the way up are given the same four names, it is in fact always innate joy. This is because the joy experienced during the ascent of the red drop is far more powerful than that during the descent of the white drop. We can experience some joy without these practices, but until the knots at the heart chakra have been loosened, it is not the complete experience of the four joys.

From the entering, abiding, and dissolving of the winds into the central channel, the drop descends and the four joys are induced, but something else happens as well. With the four joys, the four empties are experienced. Thus some scholars consider the four empties and the four joys to be the same thing.

The first empty occurs with the mind of white appearance when, from above the heart, all the winds from the right and left channels enter into the central channel and the white drop located at the crown melts and drips down. When the drop arrives at the top of the heart, our mind is filled with a brilliant white appearance like moonlight. At this stage, *empty* will occur, so-called because all the eighty conceptual thoughts and the winds that carry them dissolve.

The second empty, *very empty*, occurs when the winds from the right and left channels from the area between the heart and the secret place enter into the central channel. That brings the red drop located at the navel up toward the heart. When it touches the lower part of the heart channel knot, we experience a reddish appearance like sunset—the red increase. This stage is called *very empty* because here the mind is not only devoid of all the gross conceptual minds and their winds but also of the previous mind of white appearance and the wind that carries it.

The third empty, *great empty*, experienced with black near-attainment, occurs when the winds from above and below the heart start to move toward each other. The heart channel knot loosens, and at the center of the heart chakra the indestructible drop starts to move.

As we come closer and closer to the indestructible drop during the earlier part of this stage, we experience vacuity or blackness like a clear autumn night sky. It is called *near-attainment* because it is getting closer to clear light. This mind is called *great empty* because it is not only devoid of all gross minds and winds but also of the previous two subtle minds of white appearance and red increase and the winds that carry them.

The fourth empty, *all empty*, refers to the mind of clear light. This occurs when all the winds dissolve into the indestructible drop. The white substance from above and the red from below dissolve into the indestructible drop in the center of the heart chakra, and then all the winds dissolve into it. From there, the subtlest or primordial wind and the mind of clear light become manifest. In other words, the actual clear light will occur, completely filled with the nondual appearance of mere vacuity, free from the white, red, and black appearances. It is completely devoid of all the subtle and gross minds and winds, which is why it is called *all empty*.

The term *empty* here, it should be pointed out, does not refer to the emptiness of inherent existence but to the particular thing that each stage is empty or devoid of. Thus, with each "empty," the subtle consciousness experiences a state that is devoid of what it had experienced previously, the eighty conceptual thoughts, the white appearance, the red appearance, and the black appearance, respectively.

Clearly, too, the fullest expression of the four empties cannot occur during physical isolation, since it requires the loosening of the channel knots and the dissolution of the winds into the indestructible drop at the heart, which can only occur after verbal isolation. Nonetheless, an analogous experience of the four empties occurs here. As we will see, this experience deepens as we progress through the completion stage.

It is important to do this practice at the right time. Although the four empties and four joys are practiced together, some practitioners focus first on the four empties and then on the four joys, and some do it the other way around. The time to practice the four empties is dawn, just as daylight is starting to show. If your practice is more focused on the four joys, then cleansing the channels should be done at dusk, after the sun has set but before it actually gets dark. At a more advanced level these two must be practiced together.

THE POST-MEDITATION SESSION

There are three main activities during the post-meditation period:

+ withdrawal
+ individual investigation
+ analysis

During the post-meditation period, although all phenomena appear to us as equally empty of inherent existence, they also continue to appear as they do in our normal existence in all their varieties of shapes and sizes. The Tibetan saying that describes this state is "One taste appears as many different forms." The converse is also true: although all the phenomena that make up our post-meditative experience still appear in their myriad forms and shapes, we see them as completely empty of inherent existence. Thus it is also valid to say, "Many different forms appear as one taste."

During the post-meditation period, we need to constantly remind ourselves of what happened during the time of meditative equipoise, where we combined the realization of emptiness with the experience of great bliss. This helps us see all phenomena as a manifestation of bliss and emptiness, and in fact we refrain from any other mental activities apart from seeing everything as manifestations of bliss and emptiness. This practice of stopping other appearances is called *withdrawal*.

This is a mental consciousness rather than a sensory consciousness. Although we are not actually in the meditation session, when we start to focus on certain things such as the subtle phenomena or on emptiness and great bliss, all the sensory consciousnesses naturally withdraw from the normal objects of our senses, such as the sights, sounds, and smells around us.

During the post-meditation session we also practice what is called *individual investigation*, when we meditate on the twenty-five coarse phenomena, seeing them as manifestations of bliss and emptiness just like all other phenomena, and perceive them as the different deities we have already discussed, the hundred, twenty-five, three, or single Vajradharas. This way of seeing is called *individual investigation* because it investigates the identity of the deities and sees them as an expression of bliss and emptiness.

The final post-meditation practice is called *analysis*; it is similar to the practice of individual investigation but more thorough. Whatever phenomenon appears to us is experienced in the inseparable nature of bliss and emptiness, which causes us to enter into a state of meditative equipoise. When the object appears as a manifestation of bliss and emptiness, either the mind experiencing bliss triggers a realization of emptiness or the mind realizing emptiness triggers bliss.

When we have reached this stage, it can be quite difficult to distinguish between the actual meditation and the post-meditation. Here we can see something unique to tantra: the mental activities of the post-meditation session help us go into meditative equipoise.

TUMO PRACTICE

As we have seen, when the winds enter, abide, and dissolve into the central channel, heat is generated at the navel. Although it produces a similar result, this is not tumo practice. *Tumo*, or inner-heat practice

(Skt. *chandali*), is a technique used in mother tantras, not in father tantras like Guhyasamaja. Nevertheless, as it is a term many of you will have heard of, it is useful to give a very brief explanation of the practice.[48]

We start by visualizing at the crown chakra a flat moon disc with the letter *hum* ཧཱུྃ upside down below it, looking as though it is wearing the moon as a hat. Although *hum* is in the shape of a letter, it is actually the white drop. The crown chakra curves down in the shape of a dome. The moon disc where the *hum* is situated is in the very center of the chakra.

At the throat is the letter *ah* ཨཱཿ that is facing the right way up and is red like blood. The chakra itself is curved a little bit upward. We can picture it as though the crown and throat chakras form two umbrellas facing each other.

At the heart chakra is another *hum*, blue in color, hanging underneath the moon disc. The chakra's petals are slightly curved down. At the navel is what in Tibetan is called an *a tung*, or *short a*. It looks like a long, thin, upside-down exclamation mark, with the apex at the bottom and a *dawa* (crescent) and *tig-le* (flame drop) on top. It is like a flame, very hot and reddish in color. It is also on a moon disc.

Although the main meditation will be on the short *a* at the navel, it is very important to visualize all the mantra syllables very clearly at the beginning. When we visualize this short *a*, we must again visualize our entire mind, ourselves, our personal deity, our spiritual master, and the entire environment as being inseparable from it. The *a* is the nature of all these things. Although it is bright red and has an intense heat, at this stage it is not really blazing; the heat is in the short *a* itself. Because the knots have already been loosened in the previous meditation, the heat easily travels through our central channel, and thus we experience the four joys.

We then engage in a vase-breathing practice similar to what we saw in the kriya tantra sadhana. There are three steps. The first one is to imagine winds moving a little bit upward from the lower part of our body, through the central channel to the bottom of where the short *a* is. Then we take long gentle breaths through the nostrils and imagine that the breath passes through the central channel, moving down to above the short *a* and effectively trapping it between the two winds. We strengthen this lock by tensing our bottom muscles a little. This further constricts the space and increases the tension around the short *a*. Then we swallow a small bit of saliva without any sound, feeling it further press down on the vase at our navel, making the heat generated by the short *a* even more intense.

There are only two entrances to the central channel, at the secret place and at the crown, but Lama Tsongkhapa says that if we practice this technique with strong concentration, it is sure to make a new opening in the central channel at the navel chakra, where the winds will definitely enter. Not just that, it will also cause the short *a*, which is the nature of heat, to become hotter and actually start to burn.

During the vase-breathing meditation this flame will flare up and die out, flare up and die out. It will not stay continuously. To ignite the flame of inner heat using the vase-breathing meditation and to really experience that heat, we need to prolong the experience of that heat. The short *a* becomes a flame that is hot enough to start melting the drops above, which in turn increases the heat. As the upside-down *hum* in the nature of a white drop at the crown chakra melts, we experience the four joys as it descends through the chakras.

The way tumo is sometimes described, it might seem a wonderful shortcut to a very blissful experience, but it needs to be done only when we are at the right stage, with a firm understanding of emptiness and a strong bodhichitta motivation, otherwise it can greatly disturb the winds and hence our mental balance. It's a practice we need to approach very seriously if we wish to undertake it.

Verbal Isolation

The second stage of the six levels of the completion stage is verbal isolation, or speech isolation. It is so named because in this yoga we isolate the subtlest wind, the source of speech, from its ordinary flow and combine it inseparably with the mantra. Yangchen Gawai Lodoe says:

> By relying on the vajra repetition for the manifestation of the winds entering, abiding, and emerging to resonate (naturally) with that of the three syllables (om ah hum), the channel knots above and below the heart are loosened. Due to this the winds above and below the heart dissolve into the central channel, and consequently the wisdom of appearance arises. When that happens the practitioner moves from physical isolation to verbal isolation.[49]

The main practice in verbal isolation is a subtler type of pranayama called *vajra repetition*. This term is sometimes rendered as vajra *recitation*, and in the generation stage, it does refer to mantra recitation. But here, there is no recitation, either verbally or mentally. It is called *vajra repetition* because this practice is repeated until its goal, to loosen the channel knots at the heart chakra, is achieved. In this practice, firstly four of the five major winds are used (pervading wind is the exception), and then the practitioner moves to the five secondary branch winds that are actually a branch of the life-supporting wind.[50] Moving from the major winds to the secondary ones, the channel knots are further loosened, and there is greater access to the indestructible drop at the heart. This loosening of the knots at the heart chakra allows us to then move to the mental-isolation stage.

In the verbal-isolation stage there are three practices:

+ the mantra-drop meditation
+ the light-drop meditation
+ the substance-drop meditation

Although all three practices must be done, the actual verbal isolation is the second one, the meditation on the *light drop*, because this practice is the one that actually loosens the knots at the heart chakra, the essential feature of this stage. The first and third meditations, on the *mantra drop* and the *substance drop*, are not technically verbal-isolation practices because they are not pranayama. They do, however, support the second meditation on the light drop and, as such, are still included under the general heading of verbal isolation.

THE MANTRA-DROP MEDITATION

The first stage of verbal isolation is to meditate on the mantra drop. There are two types of mantra drops: a single syllable, such as *hum* or a short *a*, or an entire mantra garland. Here we will just discuss the short *a* (అ).

The short *a* needs to be visualized at the center of the heart chakra, where the white and red drops of the indestructible drop abide. During the physical-isolation practice we have generated ourselves into Vajradhara, with both a clear appearance and a strong identity. At the center of the indestructible drop, we visualize this short *a* as the size of a sesame seed. Due to strongly focusing on this, the winds enter, abide, and dissolve into the central channel. Although at this stage the knot at the heart chakra has not yet loosened, the mind can still enter the central channel, and we can experience the four empties and four joys as well as generate the wisdom of the inseparability of bliss and emptiness. This method will help us overcome many obscurations.

THE LIGHT-DROP MEDITATION

As we have seen, the light-drop meditation is the primary practice of the verbal isolation stage because it is the one that actually loosens the knots. To do this practice, again we have to generate into Vajradhara. Here the vajra-repetition pranayama is centered on the practice of holding the wind at the heart, but it also involves meditating on a tiny light drop at the tip of the nose and the three syllables *om ah hum*, which have the potential of a buddha's body, speech, and mind. So there are three aspects involved: the winds, the light drop, and the three letters.

Vajra-repetition pranayama has three phases, linked to the phases of our breathing: inhalation, holding the breath, and exhalation. Although we are never normally aware of it, when we breathe a kind of vibration occurs that has a certain natural sound. It is said that this sound coincides with the sounds *om ah hum*. It is neither the written words *om ah hum* nor the mental perception of the sound but a natural vibration. When we inhale, in that vibration there is a sound of *om*; when we hold the breath, in that vibration there is a sound of *ah*; and when we exhale, in that vibration there is a sound of *hum*.

We combine the light-drop meditation with vajra repetition by imagining the tiny light drop at the tip of our nose while breathing in. With the in-breath we single-pointedly concentrate on the vibration *om* passing through the central channel, forcing it past the knots in the channel. The reverberation of the *om* starts to cause the knots to loosen. It is as if we have a bundle of wires so twisted that we need to insert something into the middle to pry them apart. Here, again, it is not the mental sound *om* but a natural vibration that travels with the light drop through the knots of all the chakras. When the mind really focuses on that natural sound, certain types of energy move that actually loosen the knots.

After inhaling, when we hold our breath, there is the vibration of *ah*. This causes the knots to settle into their loosened state, rather than tighten again. Then, when we exhale, we observe the vibration *hum* rising with the light drop back through all the chakras, again forcing it through the knots and further loosening them.

Vajra repetition enables the wind in the central channel to actually move backward and forward, forcing the knots to loosen. This needs to be done again and again until all the knots, particularly the knot at the heart chakra, are loosened, and all the winds except the pervading wind enter the indestructible drop, abide there, and then dissolve into it. From that we experience the four empties and four joys, from which we experience the inseparability of great bliss and emptiness. This experience is a much higher and more profound realization than the previous one. Before, the winds merely entered the central channel, whereas now they are actually entering the area of the heart chakra.

At this stage we need to learn to practice what is called *three mixings*, which means learning to meditate while awake, asleep, and dreaming. What will happen then is that the dissolutions we can achieve while awake will continue while we sleep and even during dreamtime. Rather than slipping from a very refined state of meditation into a much grosser post-meditative mind, we now have the power to remain in this advanced state, hence greatly enhancing our progress.

THE SUBSTANCE-DROP MEDITATION

The third meditation within verbal isolation is the substance-drop meditation. It enhances the process of drawing the winds toward the indestructible drop. Here we imagine the substance drop, white and red, residing at the meeting point at the very tip of our own and the (real or imagined) consort's central channels.

It is important that before we start this meditation, the channel knots have been opened with vajra repetition so that the drops, particularly the indestructible drop, can move through the channels. Although we have been visualizing ourselves as a deity with consort, the main focus has been on the principal deity. Now we shift our focus to the actual union, either with a visualized consort or with an actual consort—that is, a real person. We will discuss this later in the next section on mental isolation.

In this meditation, through embracing the visualized or actual consort, the winds start to actually enter into the central channel and the four joys arise again. This time, though, because the practice is more advanced and the concentration is stronger, each of the four joys will be more intense.

When they occur through meditation, the white and red substances of the indestructible drop from the male and female deities' hearts move downward toward the sexual organ, where the two deities' central channels meet. Because of the joining of the channels, no substance is secreted externally.

By focusing intensely on this, we make the earlier result—the opening of the knots—far more stable. So far we have gathered the winds in the central channel, and there has been some movement as the knots loosened. Now with the substance-drop meditation we are able to hold the knots open, creating a clear channel to move the winds through.

Although the light-drop meditation is the key meditation of verbal isolation, because it actually loosens the knot at the heart chakra, the substance-drop meditation is more complex and subtle; nonetheless its job is to reinforce and strengthen the previous meditation.

Mental Isolation

THE TWO LEVELS OF MENTAL ISOLATION

By loosening the knot through the verbal-isolation practices, we move into the next stage, mental isolation.

The four empties and four joys are experienced during all three iso-lation practices, but the more advanced the practice is, the more intense and clear those experiences are. If the winds simply enter the central channel but do not abide in a particular location, which is what happens in physical isolation, the experience will not be as intense as when the winds actually abide in the central chakra.

In mental isolation the winds not only enter the central chakra but enter directly into the indestructible drop, which will only happen when the heart channel's knot is loosened due to vajra repetition. Here the experience of the empties and joys is incredibly clear and intense. Yangchen Gawai Lodoe says of mental isolation:

> It is mental isolation because it isolates the mind from the con-ceptions and the winds that serve as their mounts, causing the mind to be indivisible with bliss and emptiness.[51]

At the earlier stage of mental isolation, however, only some of the winds enter, abide, and dissolve into the indestructible drop. Others, the pervading wind in particular, do not.

There are two conditions needed to complete the mental-isolation stage. The internal condition is the vajra repetition that we have already discussed; the external condition involves practice with a con-sort or seal. There are two levels of mental isolation:

✦ mere mental isolation
✦ final mental isolation

During *mere mental isolation*, we continue with vajra repetition and at the same time practice with a wisdom seal (Skt. *prajña mudra*)—a visualized consort. By visualizing ourselves in union with the wisdom seal, bliss increases, which causes the winds to gather in the central channel at the heart level. There is even a chance that they will enter the indestructible drop.

However, the goal of this stage is to achieve the illusory body. That is the final mental isolation, and it cannot be done with a visualized consort. If we wish to achieve the illusory body in this very lifetime, we need to rely on an actual consort. Otherwise, we will have to wait until the death process.

The Action Seal

An action seal (Skt. *karma mudra*) is a real consort. We use the term "seal" to show this is something absolutely necessary, in the same way that the four basic tenets or "seals" of Buddhism—all compounded phenomena are impermanent and so on—are absolutely necessary for our grounding in Buddhism to be firm. Practicing with a visualized consort can take the practitioner almost to enlightenment, but the very fact that that is still a visualization means there is a conceptualization involved, and so there cannot be a direct realization of emptiness. By using a real consort, a direct realization of emptiness can be conjoined with the great bliss the practice brings, thus meaning the union of great bliss and emptiness is achieved, which is the stage immediately preceding enlightenment.

It is not until this stage in mental isolation that it is safe to use a consort. Before this point we are not ready, and it is extremely risky. Although I am sure Lama Tsongkhapa was ready for this practice, as an example to his followers he never sought a consort during his lifetime but instead attained the union of clear light and illusory body during the death process. Other masters have done the same. If they had taken a consort during their lifetime, they would have achieved the union of clear light and illusory body, but they chose not to do so because that might have given the wrong message to their followers, who were not ready for this practice.

If we were to reach this stage but did not want to seek the level of illusory body in this lifetime by the means of an action seal, the only occasion we could achieve it would be at the time of our death. In that case we would use the vajra repetition practice to slowly draw all the winds into the central channel and into the indestructible drop. From there, when all the appearances, all the joys, and all the empties had occurred, with the experience of the all empty we could move to the illusory body instead of moving to the bardo body as in normal death.

Choosing a consort is a very complex business. In essence, the consort must have certain qualities depending on the Dhyani Buddha family we belong to and the main deity practice we are doing. The consort should be practicing at the same level we are—or at least have an established practice in the generation stage of the same deity that we are practicing—and keep all the vows and commitments very purely.

At this stage there is a practice called *blessing the two openings*. By embracing either a wisdom or actual seal, great bliss is increased because the winds move down and increase the heat. When the drops reach the end of the sexual organ, the fourth joy, innate joy, and the fourth empty, all empty, will occur. With the mind of clear light, we meditate on emptiness.

If the consort is a wisdom seal, then that realization of emptiness will still be conceptual, because the very act of visualizing the wisdom consort means there must still be a trace of conceptuality. This is called the *simulated clear light of the mental-isolation stage*, and it occurs as we start to move to the next stage. The simulated clear light is the cooperative cause of the impure illusory body, and the wind that carries it is the main cause that brings it about.

If we rely on a real consort—an action seal—then the clear light will be without any conceptuality, which triggers a direct realization of emptiness. When this happens, we become free from the physical body. Even though we still possess the physical body, all connection to it has been cut. We are now free from all delusion and karma, which, according to the sutra system, means liberation from samsara. We are still not enlightened, but we are no longer dependent on this physical body.

When we are ready to move to the most advanced mental-isolation practice, we perform certain activities in order to increase the bliss and enhance the consciousness that realizes emptiness. These activities are called:

+ the elaborate activities
+ the non-elaborate activities
+ the very non-elaborate activities

During the elaborate activities, practitioner and consort perform activities such as wearing special masks and clothes and calling and responding to each other. Non-elaborate deeds involve fewer activities; here there is no calling and responding. With elaborate and non-elaborate activities, the practitioner uses an action seal, but with very non-elaborate activities, he or she lives in isolation and practices with a visualized consort without any of the former elaborations.[52]

The Illusory Body

At this stage in the meditation we bring not just some of the winds into the central channel but all of them, including the pervading wind, and we bring them not just into the central channel but into the indestructible drop. This causes the experience of the four empties conjoined with the four joys, with the last joy realizing all empty actually being the clear light. Yangchen Gawai Lodoe explains:

> When the minds of the three appearances—the white, the red, and the black—have ceased, the all-empty clear-light mind manifests in the central channel at the heart.[53]

Once all the winds have dissolved into the indestructible drop, the dissolutions start to appear in reverse order, and the illusory body manifests.

The main cause of the illusory body is the wind that carries the clear light that realizes all empty, and the cooperative cause is the clear light itself. That wind is called the *wind with five rays of light*, and that clear light is called the *simulated clear light*.

The illusory body is gained when we reach the final mental isolation due to the practice of vajra repetition at its most subtle level. All the winds, including the pervading wind, dissolve into the indestructible drop, and the last empty is realized by the last joy. When the wind starts to move and the reverse order of the dissolution process begins, the illusory body is accomplished. Yangchen Gawai Lodoe describes this process as being similar to "a fish leaping out of the water,"[54] where there is nothing on the surface of the water and then suddenly a fish appears. In the same way, this process is not gradual: as soon as the reverse order commences, the illusory body occurs in the same instant.

The illusory body that we arise into is a divine body. From the beginning of the generation stage, we have visualized a divine appearance, held divine pride, and performed divine activities, but here the actual divine body finally occurs. At this point in the practice a Guhyasamaja practitioner will actually arise as Guhyasamaja, with the body adorned with all the thirty-two major and eighty minor marks and the entire Guhyasamaja mandala. Because its main cause is the wind with five rays of light, this body is entirely unobstructed, in the same way that a bardo body can move anywhere at all without obstructions. It is like a dream body or a mirage, utterly unhindered by external phenomena. Although in both the generation- and completion-stage meditations, the deity has many faces, colors, and arms, at this stage the illusory body is all white with only one face and two arms.

In order to arise into the illusory body, which is a very subtle body, it is necessary to separate from the gross body. In the ordinary death process, this is exactly what the subtle consciousness of clear light and its wind do. Here the process is exactly the same. This separation does not mean that the illusory body is located in a completely different place from the gross body. It is within the gross body.

In Vajrayana there are two ways to separate the subtle clear light and its winds from the gross body. The first is the practice of the transference of consciousness (Tib. *phowa*) at the time of death in order to gain rebirth in the highest pure land. In this case, although the practice can separate the subtle mind and wind from the gross body, it does not result in the illusory body.

It is also possible to use the meditation of the final mental isolation to separate the subtle body from the gross body, which causes all the winds to enter, abide, and dissolve into the indestructible drop with the help of an actual consort. This technique will lead to the attainment of an illusory body. When we initially arise into the illusory body at the end of the final mental-isolation practice, it is within the heart chakra of the gross body. This is called the *inner awakening of the illusory body*. At this initial stage we cannot abandon the gross body because it is the result of previous karma, and the karmic connection is still there. There is also the *outer awakening of the illusory body*. This means that once we abandon the gross body, the illusory body occurs in a separate location from the previous gross body.

As long as we have not yet abandoned all the afflictions, the illusory body we arise into is still the impure illusory body. Once we have abandoned all the afflictions, it becomes the pure illusory body. We attain enlightenment with the pure illusory body.

Yangchen Gawai Lodoe has twelve similes to describe the illusory body. According to his *Paths and Grounds of Guhyasamaja*, the illusory body is:

1. *Like an illusion.* Just like an illusory person, created by a magician from a magical substance and an incantation of mantra, appears [as] a real person, an illusory body of Vajradhara with complete characteristics arising from the most subtle wind and mind appears as a real deity.

2. *Like the reflection of the moon.* Just as the reflection of the moon appears in a body of clear water, the pure and impure illusory bodies also appear to those who have the suitable disposition to see them like the clarity and stillness of open water.

3. *Like a shadow.* Just as the shadow of a body has the shape of the body but lacks flesh and bone, similarly an illusory body has a complete form but no flesh or bone because it is a wisdom body.

4. *Like a mirage.* Just as a mirage appears and disappears instantaneously, when its necessary conditions are gathered, an illusory body can also appear and disappear instantly.

5. *Like a dream body.* Just like a dream body, an illusory body can leave the coarse body of a yogi, go elsewhere to perform various activities, and return to the old body afterwards.

6. *Like an echo.* Just like an echo made by shouting into an empty cave, an illusory body exists distinctly from the old body, which arose from previous ripening actions, although the two bodies belong to the same mental continuum.

7. *Like a spirits' town.* Just as a town of gandharvas comes into existence miraculously, wherever they are born, by the power of

their karmic actions, similarly an illusory body's mandala and its residents are accomplished miraculously.

8. *Like a hallucination.* Just as in a hallucination a moon can appear as two moons to a defective perception, so an illusory body can also appear as a multitude of deities.

9. *Like a rainbow.* Just like a rainbow, an illusory body has many colors.

10. *Like lightning amidst clouds.* Just as lightning occurs from amidst the clouds, an illusory body also occurs from within the old body, and is precipitated by ripening karmic action.

11. *Like bubbles in water.* Just like bubbles bursting from water, the impure and the pure illusory bodies arise from the stirring of the subtle winds of the simulated clear light of the final isolated mind and the actual clear light of the fourth level.

12. *Like the reflection in a mirror.* Just like an image in a mirror, an illusory body has complete form.[55]

Yangchen Gawai Lodoe goes on to say that of the twelve analogies, the best is the dream body, as the others merely indicate a particular feature of the illusory body. Still, they all point to the extreme subtlety of this body, and their imagery suggests something very beautiful. With the attainment of the illusory body, our journey is almost complete, as the union of illusory body and clear light is the final stage.

Clear Light

From the illusory body, we move to the actual clear light. The clear light that occurs in the previous stage, from the final part of mental isolation up to moving into the illusory body, is called *simulated clear light.* It is so called because although it is a subtle mind realizing emptiness, it still uses a mental image to do this rather than realizing emptiness directly.

Here we practice what is called *actual clear light*, which is the clear light that realizes emptiness directly. With the illusory body, when we practice with an actual consort and thereby experience the four empties, the last stage is the innate great bliss that realizes emptiness directly without any conceptualization. That is actual clear light. At this stage, all the afflictions are abandoned, our body is a pure illusory body, and we have become an arya being, a term that refers to any being who has realized emptiness directly.

Clear light is not just a product of meditation; it is something we all possess all the time, but generally it does not manifest except at the moment of death. That is called *base clear light*. The clear light that occurs through meditation is *path clear light*; and *result clear light* is the clear light that occurs when we attain a buddha's mind through meditation.

The base clear light that all sentient beings possess does not have any object to realize; it is just the mind that is free from all conceptual thoughts. But the clear light that we are trying to manifest during the path is the mind that realizes the emptiness of inherent existence; thus it does have an object to realize. There are different levels of that clear light. There is the clear light that realizes emptiness conceptually, and there is the realization of clear light that is direct but not stable, so that we lose it when we come out of meditation. There is also the clear light that we have when we achieve enlightenment. That clear light realizes emptiness forever; that is result clear light. With result clear light there is no occasion that can be called meditative, nonmeditative, or post-meditative clear light. When we have attained full enlightenment, there is no time when our clear light does not realize emptiness.

Union

The last of the six levels of the completion stage is union, or the union of clear light and the illusory body. For the illusory body, the main cause is the subtle wind and the cooperative cause is the clear light, but for the clear light, the main cause is the basic mind and the cooperative cause is the subtle wind. With the substantial cause for clear light, we are talking about the basic mind that experiences the third empty, great empty. That mind acts as the substantial cause for the clear light, and then, when the dissolution process begins to reverse, the clear-light mind acts as the substantial cause for that basic mind. At this point the illusory body is accomplished, and the mind becomes the clear-light mind.

The texts talk about two stages of union, the learner's union and the non-learner's union. A *non-learner* here means someone who has attained the state of no-more learning—in other words, buddhahood. A *learner* then has yet to attain this state. In learner's union, we can experience the illusory body and clear light together during meditation, but this is not possible outside the session.

Learner's Union

The penultimate stage of our journey to buddhahood, learner's union, occurs before we have completely destroyed the very subtle delusions. When we experience the actual clear light for the first time, realizing emptiness directly, we start to move from the actual clear light through the reverse order of the dissolutions. At that stage, because we have abandoned all the afflictions, karmic seeds, and subtle conceptualizations of cyclic existence, also called the *subtle obscurations to liberation*,[56] the reverse order of the appearances or empties will also occur. The abandonment of all the obscurations to liberation and the illusory body is the "union" here. We have still to reach the final stage, non-learner's union, however, because although the obscurations to liberation have been abandoned, there are still very subtle obscurations—those blocking us from full enlightenment—that need to be overcome.

The texts say that the learner's union happens within one meditation session, but that does not mean that after that first session we will immediately move to non-learner's union. Each time we meditate on learner's union, the tendencies or seeds in the mindstream decrease more and more. As learners, we are not so much learning as simply habituating ourselves to what we experienced during that initial meditation.

Non-Learner's Union

When those karmic tendencies are exhausted completely, the next step is the non-learner's union. Although it might take a long time to destroy the subtle delusions that remain as seeds in the mindstream, moving from learner's union to non-learner's union happens very quickly. It is sometimes said that the meditation might start at dawn, move through the stages during the day, and result in the attainment of complete enlightenment at dusk.

To move from learner's union to non-learner's union, we need to have four vajras. A *vajra* here is not the hand implement but rather a stage of the consort yoga. The first vajra is the joining of the ends of our central channel with the consort's while embracing. This is called the *channel vajra*. When the sexual organs of the male and female deities meet, the winds, particularly the downward-voiding winds, are held at the place of meeting. This is known as the *wind vajra*.

Through the channels being joined, the energy moves and the drops descend, increasing the bliss and the number of drops coming together at the joining of the channels. This continuous coming together of the drops is called the *drops vajra*. Finally, the movement of the drops causes the experience of great bliss realizing emptiness, which is called the *vajra of great bliss and emptiness*.

When the non-learner's union has finally been reached—when we have become a buddha—this attainment is shown by seven features. They are:

+ Our complete sambhogakaya has the thirty-two major and eighty minor marks of a buddha.
+ Our complete sambhogakaya is embracing a wisdom seal.
+ Our mind always remains in a state of great bliss.
+ Our bliss is always mixed with the cognition of emptiness.
+ Our mind never wavers from great compassion for all sentient beings.
+ Our body's continuum never ceases.
+ Our emanations pervade the universe ceaselessly performing activities for the benefit of others.

The first feature we show when we have achieved non-learner's union is that we have a complete sambhogakaya, the enjoyment body of a buddha, with its thirty-two major and eighty minor marks. We would have had many of these signs during the learner's stage, but an actual buddha's body is different from the body we have while we are on the path. It is only when we reach buddhahood that all of the major and minor marks will be present.

The second feature is that the complete sambhogakaya embraces the wisdom seal. The non-learner's body is constantly in union with the consort, which represents the fact that the enlightened being is always inseparable from the wisdom realizing emptiness.

The third feature is that the mind always remains in the state of great bliss. There is no time great bliss is not experienced, and this is always mixed with the cognition of emptiness, which is the fourth feature.

The fifth is that the mind never wavers from great compassion for all sentient beings, and the sixth is that the continuum of the body never ceases. After attaining the union of illusory body and clear light, at no time does that particular body cease, because the causes that created it are not those that produced our previous, ordinary body. Our current body deteriorates due to causes and conditions; a buddha's body never will.

The final feature is that our emanations pervade the universe, ceaselessly performing activities for the benefit of others. Although we are constantly in the meditative state realizing emptiness that experiences great bliss, there are countless nirmanakayas covering entire universes going out to benefit sentient beings.

No-More Learning

In the Sutrayana system there are five paths we must progress through to become a buddha: the path of accumulation, the path of preparation, the path of seeing, the path of meditation, and the path of no-more learning.

Having actualized the non-learner's union, completing the union of clear light and illusory body, we have attained the absolute final goal of the entire Buddhist path, buddhahood. We are a buddha. There is nothing more we need to do, nothing more we need to develop, nothing more we need to purify. We are there. This is why this last of the five stages is called *the path of no-more learning*. Now we are a perfect instrument for benefitting each and every sentient being in the most profound way possible.

It is interesting, in summary, to compare the stages of highest yoga tantra with these five paths, depicted in table 6.

The generation stage correlates to the first of the five paths, the path

TABLE 6. THE STAGES OF HIGHEST YOGA TANTRA AND THE FIVE PATHS[57]

Stages	Levels of Stages	Location of the Dissolution of Winds in Central Channel	Sutra Paths
generation stage	coarse stage of generation	imaginary dissolution	path of accumulation
	subtle stage of generation		
completion stage	physical isolation	at lower opening	path of preparation
	verbal isolation	at heart	
	mental isolation		
	impure illusory body	at indestructible drop at heart (some winds)	
	actual clear light		path of seeing
	learner's union		path of meditation
buddhahood	non-learner's union	at indestructible drop at heart (all winds)	path of no-more learning

of accumulation. Here we have not only renunciation and wisdom but bodhichitta as well. The completion stage correlates to the next three paths—of preparation, seeing, and meditation. With the learner's union, we have a direct realization of emptiness, but the subtlest obscurations to omniscience still need to be overcome, and so this is the path of meditation.

Only when we have completely purified all the subtle obscurations to omniscience are we able to bring the consciousness into the indestructible drop at the heart. At that time, we attain our final goal: non-learner's union, the path of no-more learning, buddhahood, omniscience, enlightenment.

* * *

In this book I have only just touched the surface of Vajrayana. Each tantric practice has its own deep complexities; it would be impossible to thoroughly explain the significance and method of each practice in a book of this length. Although the vision of tantra I have presented here might seem very complex, it is as simple as I could make it without diluting its essence. If you are serious about taking on a Vajrayana practice, or enhancing one you already have, I urge you to search for more information and take more teachings.

For most of us, the difficulty is engaging in the meditations. We learn a bit here and a bit there, but when we try to actually begin our meditation practice, we are unsure of how to start. The vastness of the practice, the seeming impossibility of the visualizations, and the esoteric language of the texts all make a tantric practice seem quite daunting. But in fact, we should be inspired, not daunted. When we have taken our first initiation and sit in front of the altar at home with the meditation manual open to page 1, we have before us a road map to enlightenment. There is nothing more we need in order to shatter the limiting conceptions of ordinariness currently dominating our lives and to turn our mind toward its ultimate potential.

The vital point, however, is not how profound our intellectual understanding of a Dharma subject is but how much we have integrated Dharma into our lives. By sincerely taking the teachings of Buddha into our hearts, we can transform our lives and make ourselves better people. By taking on a Vajrayana commitment and doing it as sincerely as we can, we are doing just that. It might seem daunting, it might seem that this is a practice that is way beyond our comprehension and ability, but if we stick at it with a good heart, something will certainly change.

As you have doubtlessly gathered from this book and whatever else you have learned about tantra, its profundity and its very esoteric nature means its subtleties will be hidden from us until we dig deeply into it through diligently practicing it. That is exactly what I urge you to do. This is definitely the quickest way out of the muddled state we call samsara and the quickest way to transform the mind from one of self-interest to selflessness. By visualizing ourselves as an enlightened being, we become an enlightened being. This is definitely possible, but even in the very early stages of our practice, our heavy burden of the sense of worthlessness and ordinariness is shifted, and we are able to achieve a profound transformation. We desperately need this transformation; the world desperately needs this transformation.

APPENDIX 1
THE INSEPARABILITY OF THE GURU AND AVALOKITESHVARA

A Source of All Powerful Attainments

By Tenzin Gyatso,
His Holiness the Fourteenth Dalai Lama

Translation and annotation by Sharpa Tulku and Brian Beresford

Introduction

To my spiritual master Avalokiteshvara,
The full-moon-like essence of the buddhas' vast compassion
And the radiant white nectar of their all-inspiring strength,
I pay my deep respect.
I shall now disseminate to all other beings the standard practice
   of this profound yoga.

The root of every inspiration and powerful attainment (*siddhi*) lies
solely with the spiritual master (*lama* or *guru*). As such he has been
praised in both sutras and tantras more than once. He is of fundamental importance because the basis for achieving everlasting happiness is requesting him to teach the undistorted path. Thinking of him
as being inseparable from the specific meditational deity with whom
you feel a special affinity, you should visualize the two as one.

The vitality of the Mahayana tradition comes from compassion,
love, and the altruistic aspiration to attain enlightenment (*bodhichitta*)
in order to effectively help all creatures become free from their suffering. Moreover, the importance of compassion is emphasized throughout all stages of development. Therefore, if you wish to combine
Avalokiteshvara, the meditational deity of compassion, with your own
root guru, first gather fine offerings in a suitable place. Sitting on a
comfortable seat in an especially virtuous state of mind, take refuge,
generate an enlightened motive of the awakening mind, and meditate
on the four immeasurable thoughts.

The Preliminary Practices

REFUGE

Namo Gurubhyah	In the spiritual masters, I take refuge;
Namo Buddhaya	In the Awakened One, I take refuge;
Namo Dharmaya	In his Truth, I take refuge;
Namo Sanghaya	In the spiritual aspirants, I take refuge.

GENERATING BODHICHITTA

In the Supreme Awakened One, his Truth, and the Spiritual
   Community,
I seek refuge until becoming enlightened.
By the merit from practicing giving and other perfections,
May I accomplish full awakening for the benefit of all.

THE FOUR IMMEASURABLE THOUGHTS

May all sentient beings possess happiness and the cause
   of happiness.
May all sentient beings be parted from suffering and the cause
   of suffering.
May all sentient beings never be parted from the happiness
   that has no suffering.
May all sentient beings abide in equanimity without attachment
   or aversion for near or far.

Recite these prayers three times each.

The Actual Practice

PURIFICATION OF PLACE
May the surface of the earth in every direction
Be stainless and pure, without roughness or fault,
As smooth as the palm of a child's soft hand
And as naturally polished as lapis lazuli.

May the material offerings of gods and humans,
Both those set before me and those visualized
Like a cloud of the peerless offerings of Samantabhadra,*
Pervade and encompass the vastness of space.

*Om namo bhagavate vajra sara pramardane tathagataya / arhate samyak
sambuddhaya / tadyatha / om vajre vajre / maha vajre / maha teja vajre /
maha vidya vajre / maha bodhichitta vajre / maha bodhi mando pasam
kramana vajre / sarva karma avarana visho dhana vajre soha*

Recite this purification mantra three times.

By the force of the truth of the Three Jewels of Refuge,
By the firm inspiration from all bodhisattvas and buddhas,
By the power of the buddhas who have fully completed their
    collections of both good merit and insight,
By the might of the void, inconceivable and pure,
May all of these offerings be hereby transformed into their actual
    nature of voidness.

In this way bless the surroundings and the articles of offering.

---

*Samantabhadra is one of the eight bodhisattvas of the Mahayana lineage. He is
famed for the extensiveness of his offerings made to the buddhas of the ten directions.

Guru Yoga and Accumulating Merit

VISUALIZING THE MERIT FIELD
Visualize the spiritual master in the manner of the three sattvas: samayasattva (commitment being), jñanasattva (wisdom being), and samadhisattva (concentration being).

In the space of the dharmakaya of great spontaneous bliss,
In the midst of billowing clouds of magnificent offerings,
Upon a sparkling, jeweled throne supported by eight snow lions,*
On a seat composed of a lotus in bloom, the sun and the moon,
Sits supreme exalted Avalokiteshvara, great treasure of compassion,
Assuming the form of a monk wearing saffron-colored robes.

O my Vajradhara master, kind in all three ways, holy Losang
    Tenzin Gyatso,
Endowed with a glowing fair complexion and a radiant smiling face,
Your right hand at your heart in a gesture expounding Dharma
Holds the stem of one white lotus that supports a book and sword;
Your left hand resting in meditative pose holds a thousand-spoked
    wheel.
You are clothed in the three saffron robes of a monk,
And are crowned with the pointed, golden hat of a pandit.**
Your aggregates, sensory spheres, senses, and objects, as well as
    your limbs,

---

*Four of the eight snow lions look upward, providing protection from interferences from above. Four gaze downward, protecting from interferences from below.
**The three robes stand for the three higher trainings in ethics, meditative stabilization, and discriminating wisdom. The golden hat of a pandit symbolizes pure morality. Its point stands for penetrative wisdom. A pandit is a master of the five major branches of knowledge: art, medicine, grammar, reasoning, and the inner, or Buddhist, sciences.

Are a mandala complete with the five buddhas and their consorts,
Male and female bodhisattvas, and the wrathful protectors.

Encircled by a halo of five brilliant colors,*
My master is seated in full vajra posture,
Sending forth a network of cloud-like self-emanations
To tame the minds of all sentient beings.

Within his heart sits Avalokiteshvara, a wisdom being,
With one face and four arms.
His upper two hands are placed together,
His lower two hands hold a crystal rosary and white lotus.**
He is adorned with jeweled ornaments and heavenly raiment.
Over his left shoulder an antelope skin is draped,***
And cross-legged he is seated on a silver moon and lotus.
The white syllable *hrih*, a concentration being at his heart,
Emits brilliant colored light in all the ten directions.

On my master's brow is a white *om*,
Within his throat, a red *ah*,
At his heart, a blue *hum*
From which many lights shine out in myriad directions,
Inviting the Three Jewels of Refuge to dissolve into him,

*The five colors—red, blue, yellow, green, and white—are associated with the five Dhyani Buddhas.

**The beads on the crystal rosary held by Avalokiteshvara symbolize sentient beings. The action of turning the beads indicates that he is drawing them out of their misery in cyclic existence and leading them into the state beyond sorrow (*nirvana*). The white lotus symbolizes his pure state of mind.

***The antelope is known to be very kind and considerate toward its offspring and is therefore a symbol for bodhichitta, the cultivation of a kind and compassionate attitude toward others.

Transforming him into the collected essence of the objects
of refuge.

In this manner visualize the spiritual master.

Accumulating Merit

The Seven-Limb Prayer
Prostrating
Your liberating body is fully adorned with all the signs of a buddha;*
Your melodious speech, complete with all sixty rhythms, flows with-
out hesitation;
Your vast, profound mind filled with wisdom and compassion is
beyond all conception;
I prostrate to the wheel of these three secret adornments of your
body, speech, and mind.

Offering
Material offerings of my own and those of others,
The actual objects and those that I visualize,
Body and wealth, and all virtues amassed throughout the three
times,
I offer to you upon visualized oceans of clouds like Samantabhadra's
offerings.

Confessing
My mind being oppressed by the stifling darkness of ignorance,
I have done many wrongs against reason and vows.

---

*There are thirty-two major and eighty minor signs that indicate the attainments
of an enlightened being.

Whatever mistakes I have made in the past,

With a deep sense of regret I pledge never to repeat them

And without reservation I confess everything to you.

Rejoicing

From the depths of my heart,

I rejoice in the enlightening deeds of the sublime masters

And in the virtuous actions past, present, and future

Performed by myself and all others as well,

And by ordinary and exalted beings of the three sacred traditions.*

Requesting

I request you to awaken every living being

From the sleep of ordinary and instinctive defilements

With the divine music of the Dharma's pure truth,

Resounding with the melody of profoundness and peace

And in accordance with the dispositions of your various disciples.

Entreating

I entreat you to firmly establish your feet upon the indestructible
   vajra throne

In the indissoluble state of *evam*,

Until every sentient being gains the calm breath of joy in the state
   of final realization,

Unfettered by the extremes of worldliness or tranquil liberation.

Dedicating

I dedicate fully my virtuous actions of all the three times,

So that I may receive continuous care from a master

*The three sacred traditions of Buddhism are the vehicles of the shravakas, pratyeka-
buddhas, and bodhisattvas.

And attain full enlightenment for the benefit of all
Through accomplishing my prayers, the supreme deed of
    Samantabhadra.

The Mandala Offering

By the virtue of offering to you, assembly of buddhas visualized
    before me,
This mandala built on a base, resplendent with flowers, saffron
    water, and incense,
Adorned with Mount Meru and the four continents, as well as the
    sun and the moon,
May all sentient beings share in its boundless effects.

This offering I make of a precious jeweled mandala,
Together with other pure offerings and wealth
And the virtues we have collected throughout the three times
With our body, speech, and mind.

O my masters, my yidams, and the Three Precious Jewels,
I offer all to you with unwavering faith.
Accepting these out of your boundless compassion,
Send forth to me waves of your inspiring strength.
Om idam guru ratna mandalakam niryatayami

Thus make the offering of the mandala together with the seven-limb prayer.

The Main Deity Practice

Blessings by the Master

From the *hrih* in the heart of Avalokiteshvara,
Seated in the heart of my venerable master,

Flow streams of nectar and rays of five colors
Penetrating the crown of my head,
Eliminating all obscurations and endowing me with both
Common and exclusive powerful attainments.

*Om ah guru vajradhara vagindra sumati shasana dhara samudra shri
bhadra sarva siddhi hum hum*

Recite the mantra of the spiritual master as many times as possible.*

THE PRAYER OF THE GRADUATED PATH
Bestow on me your blessings to be devoted to my master
With the purest thoughts and actions, gaining confidence that you,
O compassionate holy master, are the basis of temporary and ever-
lasting bliss,
For you elucidate the true path free from all deception
And embody the totality of refuges past number.

Bestow on me your blessings to live a life of Dharma
Undistracted by the illusory preoccupations of this life,
For well I know that these leisures and endowments
Can never be surpassed by countless treasures of vast wealth,
And that this precious form once attained cannot endure,
For at any moment of time it may easily be destroyed.

Bestow on me your blessings to cease actions of non-virtue
And accomplish wholesome deeds, by being always mindful
Of the causes and effects from kind and harmful acts,

---

*The name mantra of His Holiness the Dalai Lama contains these words: Ngawang
(Skt: *vagindra*), lord of speech; Losang (Skt. *sumati*), excellent mind; Tenzin (Skt.
shasanadhara), upholder of the Buddha's teachings; Gyatso (Skt. *samudra*), ocean.

While revering the Three Precious Jewels as the ultimate source of
    refuge
And most trustworthy protection from the unendurable fears of
    unfortunate rebirth states.

Bestow on me your blessings to practice the three higher trainings,*
Motivated by firm renunciation gained from the clear comprehension
That even the prosperity of the lord of the devas
Is merely a deception, like a siren's alluring spell.

Bestow on me your blessings to master the oceans of practice,
Cultivating immediately the supreme enlightened motivation,
By reflecting on the predicament of all mother sentient beings,
Who have nourished me with kindness from beginningless time
And now are tortured while ensnared within one extreme or other,
Either on the wheel of suffering or in tranquil liberation.

Bestow on me your blessings to generate the yoga
Combining mental quiescence with penetrative insight,
In which the hundred-thousand-fold splendor of voidness, forever
    free from both extremes,**
Reflects without obstruction in the clear mirror of the immutable
    meditation.

Bestow on me your blessings to observe in strict accordance
All the vows and words of honor that form the root of powerful
    attainments,

*The three higher trainings are ethics (shila), meditative concentration (samadhi),
and discriminating wisdom (prajña).
**The two extremes are the beliefs in either true self-existence or nonexistence.
The middle way (madhyamaka) shows a path that is neither of these.

Having entered through the gate of the extremely profound tantra
By the kindness of my all-proficient master.

Bestow on me your blessings to attain within this lifetime
The blissful mahamudra of the union of body and wisdom,*
Through severing completely my all-creating karmic energy
With wisdom's sharp sword of the nonduality of bliss and emptiness.

*Having made requests in this way for the development in your
mindstream of the entire paths of sutra and tantra, and thus having done
a glance meditation on them, now recite the six-syllable mantra in
connection with the merging of the spiritual master into your heart.*

THE MERGING OF THE SPIRITUAL MASTER
My supreme master, requested in this way,
Now blissfully descends through the crown of my head
And dissolves in the indestructible point
At the center of my eight-petalled heart.
Now my master re-emerges on a moon and lotus.
In his heart sits Avalokiteshvara, within whose heart is the
    letter *hrih*
Encircled by a rosary of the six-syllable mantra, the source from
    which streams of nectar flow,
Eliminating all obstacles and every disease
And expanding my knowledge of the scriptural and insight
    teachings of the Buddha.

---

*The Great Seal (*mahamudra, chagya chenpo*) of the union of body and wisdom
(*yuganaddha, zungjug*) is the unity of the clear light (*prabhasvara, osel*) and the illusory body (*mayakaya, gyulu*), The illusory body is the finest physical body, a combination of energy [or wind] (*vayu, lung*) and consciousness (*chitta, sem*). The clear
light is the wisdom of the nonduality of bliss and voidness.

Thus, I receive the entire blessings of the victorious ones and their
   children,
And radiant lights again shine forth
To cleanse away defects from all beings and their environment.

In this way I attain the supreme yogic state,
Transforming every appearance, sound, and thought
Into the three secret ways of the exalted ones.*

Recitation of the Mantra of Avalokiteshvara

After completing the above, recite the six-syllable mantra, Om mani padme hum, *as
many times as possible. Upon conclusion, recite once the hundred-syllable mantra of
Vajrasattva.*

*Om vajrasattva samaya manupalaya vajrasattva tenopatita dridho me
bhava sutoshyo me bhava suposhyo me bhava anu rakto me bhava sarva
siddhim me prayacha sarva karma sucha me chittam shriyam kuru hum
ha ha ha ha hoh bhagavan sarva tathagata vajra ma me muncha vajra
bhava maha samaya sattva ah hum phat*

Dedication

In the glorious hundred-thousand-fold radiance of the youthful
   moon of wholesome practice,
From the blue jasmine garden of Victorious Treasure Mind's method
   of truth**

*The three secret ways of the exalted ones are: (a) viewing all surroundings as a bliss-
ful abode (mandala) and all beings as manifestations of deities, (b) hearing all sound
as mantra, and (c) intuitively knowing everything to be empty of true existence.
**"Victorious Treasure Mind" is a name given to Manjushri, the meditational deity
embodying discriminating wisdom. His method of truth is the direct cognition of
voidness.

May the seeds of explanation and accomplishment germinate and
    flower across this vast earth;
May the ensuing auspiciousness beautify everything until the limit
    of the universe.

By flying high above the three realms
The never-vanishing great jeweled banner of religious and
    secular rule,*
Laden with millions of virtues and perfect accomplishments:
May myriad wishes for benefit and bliss pour down.
Having banished afar the dark weight of this era's degeneration
Across the extent of the earth sapphire held by a celestial maiden,
May all living creatures overflow with spontaneous gaiety and joy
In the significant encompassing brilliance of happiness and bliss.

In short, O protector, by the power of your affectionate care,
May I never be parted from you throughout the rosaries of my lives.
May I proceed directly, with an ease beyond effort,
Unto the great city of unification, the all-powerful cosmic state
    itself.

*Having offered prayers of dedication in this way, also recite others such as the "Yearn-
ing Prayer of Samantabhadra's Activity" or "The Prayer of the Virtuous Beginning,
Middle, and End."** Upon conclusion recite the following prayer.*

---

*Religious and secular rule refers to the form of government in Tibet prior to 1959.
**Bhadracharyapranidhana (Zangpo chope monlam) is the "Yearning Prayer of Saman-
tabhadra's Activity." Togtama by Je Tsongkhapa is "The Prayer of the Virtuous
Beginning, Middle, and End."

Conclusion

By the force of the immaculate compassion of the victorious ones
    and their sons,
May everything adverse be banished for eternity throughout the
    universe.
May all favorable omens become increasingly auspicious,
And may whatever is of virtue in the round of this existence or in
    tranquil liberation
Flourish and grow brighter like a new moon waxing full.

*This has been written at the repeated request of the assistant cabinet minis-
ter, Mr. Shankawa Gyurme Sonam Tobgyal, who, with sincere faith and
offerings, asked me to write a simple and complete sadhana of the inseparability of Avalokiteshvara and myself. This devotion contains a short glance
meditation on the entire graduated path and the mantras of the master and
Avalokiteshvara. Although it is improper for me to write such a devotion
about myself, waves of inspiration of the buddhas can be received from ordinary beings just as relics can come from a dog's tooth.* Therefore, I have
composed this with the hope of benefiting a few faithful disciples.*

The Buddhist monk
Ngawang Losang Tenzin Gyatso
maintaining the title of Holder of the White Lotus (Avalokiteshvara)

---

*Once in Tibet a very devout woman asked her son, who journeyed on trading expe-
ditions to India, to bring back for her a relic of Buddha. Although the son went three
times, each time he forgot the promised relic. Not wanting to disappoint his mother
again, he picked up a dog's tooth as he was nearing home on his last journey and
reverently presented that to her. She was overjoyed and placed the tooth upon the
family altar. She then made many devotions to the "holy tooth" and, to the amaze-
ment of her son, from the tooth came several true relics.

Appendix 2
The Six Deities within the Nyungné Practice

Taken from *Nyung Nä: The Means of Achievement of the Eleven-Face Great Compassionate One.*[*]

How to Meditate on the Self-Generation

1. The Ultimate Deity

Contemplating as follows is the meditation on the ultimate deity:

om svabhava shuddha sarva dharma svabhava shuddho ham

The nature of myself, the deity to be meditated upon, and all phenomena are in the essence of one taste in emptiness.

2. The Deity of Sound

From the sphere of emptiness the aspect of the mantra, *om mani padme hum*, resounds, pervading the realm of space.

3. The Deity of Syllables

Contemplating as follows is the meditation on the deity of syllables:

*Seventh Dalai Lama, *Nyung Nä: The Means of Achievement of the Eleven-Face Great Compassionate One* (Boston: Wisdom Publications, 1995), pp. 74–81.

My mind, in the aspect of the undifferentiated suchness of myself and the deity, becomes a moon mandala, upon which the very aspect of the tone of the mantra resounding in space is set down having the form of written syllables (the sounds and the written letters mixing), like very pure mercury adhering to grains of gold.

4. The Deity of Form

Contemplating as follows is the meditation on the deity of form:

The syllables transform into a thousand-petalled lotus, as brilliant as refined gold, marked at the center by the mantra, *om mani padme hum.* From the tips of multicolored light rays emitted from the moon, lotus, and mantra, innumerable holy bodies of Arya Avalokiteshvara spread out, pervading all the realms of space. Great clouds of miraculously emanated offerings are beautifully offered to the buddhas and their children. From yet another great emanated cloud, a continuous rain of nectar descends, extinguishing the fires of the suffering of all migrators of the hells and other realms. They are satisfied with bliss (and become Avalokiteshvara). Then the light rays, along with the bodies of the deity, return and enter into one's own mind in the aspect of the moon mandala, lotus, and mantra garland.

These transform into a multicolored lotus and moon seat, upon which oneself arises as Avalokiteshvara with a white-colored body in the prime of youth and radiating rays of light. Of the eleven faces, the root face is white; the right, green; and the left, red. Above that, the central face is green; the right, red; and the left, white. Above that, the central face is red; the right, white; and the left, green. They also have long narrow eyes and smiling expressions. Above these is a wrathful black face with bared fangs and wrathful wrinkles, a third eye, and orange hair standing upright. On the crown is a peaceful red face with a crown protrusion, having a chaste aspect, devoid of ornaments, with its own neck.

The first two hands are folded at the heart (and hold a jewel). The second right hand holds a rosary; the third eliminates hunger and thirst of the hungry ghosts by sending down a stream of nectar from the mudra of granting sublime realizations; the fourth holds a wheel. The second left hand holds a golden lotus with a stem, the third holds a water vessel, and the fourth holds a bow and arrow.

The remaining nine hundred and ninety-two hands, as soft as lotus petals, are in the mudra of granting sublime realizations. In the palm of every hand is an eye. The hands do not extend above the crown protrusion nor below the knees.

An antelope skin covers the left breast, and there is a lower garment of fine cloth. The waist is endowed with a golden belt adorned with jewels; (the head of the wrathful face) is beautified with a garland of orange hair. He has a jeweled crown, earrings, necklace, armlets, bracelets, and anklets, wears garments of various-colored silks, and radiates rays of white light.

5. The Deity of Mudra
At the crown of the central head is a white *om*, at the throat, a red *ah*, and at the heart, a blue *hum*. Upon the moon disk at the heart is a white *hrih*.

Then, say the following mantra five times while touching and blessing the heart, brow, throat, and tops of the right and left shoulders with one's hands in the commitment mudra of the lotus family. This is the deity of the mudra.

om padma udbhavaya svaha

6. The Deity of Sign
Invocation and Absorption of the Wisdom Beings
Then, invoke the wisdom beings saying:
Light rays radiate from the *hrih* at the heart, invoking from their natural abode Arya Avalokiteshvara surrounded by the entire assembly of buddhas and bodhisattvas.

*om arya lokeshvara saparivara vajra samaya jah jah
jah hum bam hoh*

Contemplate:
They become nondual with oneself, the commitment being.

Empowerment
Again, light rays radiate from the *hrih* at one's heart, invoking the empowering deities: the five buddha families with Amitabha as their principal, together with their retinues.

Present offerings while saying:

*om pancha kula saparivara argham (padyam / pushpe / dhupe / aloke / gandhe
/ naivedya / shabda) praticcha svara*

"All tathagatas, please bestow the empowerment upon me."

Requested thus, the Goddess Dressed in White and the others who are emitted from the tathagatas' hearts hold aloft vases filled with nectar and say:

> Just as at the very time of birth,
> The devas offered ablution (to the Buddha),

So do I, with pure divine water,
Offer ablution to the holy body.

om sarva tathagatha abhishekata samaya shri ye hum

The bestow the empowerment. Thereby, the entire body is filled and all defilements are purified. From a transformation of the excesses water remaining on the crown, the head becomes adorned with [red] Amitabha on the crown, who is in the very nature of one's guru, [blue] Akshobhya on the forehead, [yellow] Ratnasambhava behind the right ear, [white] Vairochana at the back, and [green] Amoghasiddhi behind the left ear.

Contemplate that:
On a moon cushion at one's heart is the exalted wisdom being. Arya Avalokiteshvara, with a white body, one face, and two hands. The right hand is in the mudra of bestowing sublime realizations, and the left holds a lotus (at his heart).

The moon cushion at his heart is marked by the concentration being, a white *hrih*.

[Then follows offering to the self-generation and mantra recitation.]

NOTES

1. The four noble truths are: the truth of suffering, the truth of the cause of suffering, the truth of the cessation of suffering, and the truth of the path leading to the cessation of suffering. The thirty-seven aspects of enlightenment are: the four mindfulnesses, the four complete abandonments, the four states of *samadhi*, the five faculties, the five powers, the seven branches of the path to enlightenment, and the noble eightfold path. The twelve links of dependent origination are: ignorance, karma, consciousness, name and form, sense bases, contact, feeling, clinging, craving, existence, birth, and aging and death. See Geshe Tashi Tsering, *The Four Noble Truths* (Boston: Wisdom Publications, 2005).

2. A *bodhisattva* is someone who possesses *bodhichitta*, the mind that spontaneously wishes to attain enlightenment in order to benefit others. The six perfections are the perfections of generosity, morality, patience, joyous perseverance, concentration, and wisdom. See Geshe Tashi Tsering, *The Awakening Mind* (Boston: Wisdom Publications, 2008), pp. 109–43.

3. From *Visualizing Yourself as a Deity*, Lama Yeshe Wisdom Archive website, lamayeshe.com.

4. There are many books on the lamrim, but the seminal one and the source of so many teachings by Gelug masters is Lama Tsongkhapa's *Great Treatise on the Stages of the Path to Enlightenment* (*Lamrim Chenmo*).

5. Panchen Lama I, Losang Chokyi Gyaltsen, *Guru Puja*, vv. 44–46.

6. Quoted in Panchen Sonam Dragpa, *An Overview of Buddhist Tantra* (Dharamsala: The Library of Tibetan Works and Archives, 1996), p. 67.

7. The ten categories or outer principles that a vajra master should know are: (1) how to meditate on the mandala with and without form, (2) how to maintain meditative stabilization as the deity within the mandala, (3) how to do the various mudras for offering adornments to the deities, (4) how to perform ritual dance, (5) how to assume a variety of postures such as the vajra position, (6) how to recite mantras, (7) how to conduct peaceful, increasing, powerful, and wrathful fire pujas, (8) how to make outer, inner, and secret offerings, (9) how to perform peaceful, increasing, powerful, and wrathful activities, and (10) how

to conclude rituals. See Lama Zopa Rinpoche, *The Heart of the Path* (Boston: Lama Yeshe Wisdom Archive, 2009), pp. 33–37.

8. A self-initiation is a highest yoga tantra meditation practice that one can perform after one has taken initiation into a deity and completed a long retreat and fire puja.

9. Dragpa, *Overview of Buddhist Tantra*, p. 68.

10. A seed syllable is a Sanskrit letter used in tantric visualizations, arising out of emptiness, from which the tantric deity in turn arises.

11. The five lay vows are often given at the same time as formal refuge. These vows are to be taken for life. They are to avoid: killing, stealing, sexual misconduct, lying, and taking intoxicants. A student can usually choose whether to take one, more, or all five.

12. This is sometimes given the previous day, and in some initiations this counts as a separate initiation.

13. The five aggregates (Skt. *skandha*) are the five mental and physical constituents that make up a person: form, feeling, discrimination, compositional factors, and consciousness.

14. The Dhyani Buddhas represent the five buddha families, which in turn represent the five primordial wisdoms and the five aggregates. They are: white Vairochana, mirror-like wisdom (Skt. *adarshajñana*) and form; red Amitabha, wisdom of analysis (*pratyavekshanajñana*) and discrimination; yellow Ratnasambhava, wisdom of equality (*samatajñana*) and feeling; green Amoghasiddhi, wisdom of achieving activities (*krityanushtanajñana*) and compositional factors; and blue Akshobhya, dharmadhatu wisdom (*dharmadhatujñana*) and consciousness.

15. For an explanation of the bodhisattva vows, see Tsering, *The Awakening Mind*, pp. 92–97, or Khen Rinpoche Lama Lhundrup's *The Bodhisattva Vows* available at lamayeshe.com. For more on tantric vows, see Lama Tsongkhapa's *Tantric Ethics*, trans. Gareth Sparham (Boston: Wisdom Publications, 2005).

16. This is a commitment for specific practices such as a *nyungné* or a retreat rather than daily practice.

17. Modified from *Destiny Fulfilled*, from *The Life and Teachings of Tsong Khapa*, edited by Robert Thurman (Dharamsala: Library of Tibetan Works and Archives, 1982), p. 42.

18. The three poisonous minds are ignorance, aversion, and attachment, so-called because they are the three main delusions that keep us trapped in samsara.

19. The original translation by Brian Beresford et al. accompanied by the Tibetan text appears in *Aryashura's Aspiration, and A Meditation on Compassion*, published by the Library of Tibetan Works and Archives in 1978. A commentary on this sadhana appears in Lama Thubten Yeshe, *Becoming the Compassion Buddha: Tantric Meditation for Everyday Life*, edited by Robina Courtin (Boston: Wisdom Publications, 2003).

20. Lapis lazuli is a semiprecious gem, deep blue in color and usually highly polished.

21. The lotus, rising through the mire of a swamp, symbolizes the purity of the bodhisattva who rises above the bonds of cyclic existence, uncontaminated by the confusion of the world. The moon symbolizes the conventional enlightened motivation of bodhichitta. The sun symbolizes the ultimate wisdom of bodhichitta: the direct cognition of voidness, the true mode of existence.

22. The white lotus symbolizes the pure nature of the discriminating wisdom of penetrative insight into voidness. The knowledge of this is symbolized by the book of scripture resting on the lotus together with the flaming sword of total awareness that cuts through the root of ignorance. The scripture is one of the perfection of wisdom (*prajñaparamita*) sutras.

23. Lama Govinda, *The Way of the White Clouds* (Boston: Shambhala, 1988), p. 54.

24. Modified from Yanchen Gawai Lodoe, *Paths and Grounds of Guhyasamaja According to Arya Nagarjuna* (Dharamsala: The Library of Tibetan Works and Archives, 1995), p. 19.

25. For a summary of these dissolutions, along with the external and internal signs that occur and the deities of the Guhyasamaja mandala related to them, see table 3 in chapter 6. See also Lati Rinbochay and Jeffrey Hopkins, *Death, Intermediate State, and Rebirth in Tibetan Buddhism* (Ithaca: Snow Lion Publications, 1979).

26. The descriptions of the intermediate state in this section are primarily drawn from chapter 3 of Vasubandhu's *Treasury of Higher Knowledge* (*Abhidharmakosha*).

27. There are three realms in Buddhist cosmology: the *desire realm* we live in; the *form realm*, where beings are in very advanced states of concentration; and the *formless realm*, where the concentration is even more advanced and beings have no corporeal form at all.

28. Lodoe, *Paths and Grounds of Guhyasamaja*, p. 42.

29. There are two sets of obscurations (Skt. *avarana*), those that block us from liberation—that is, our mental afflictions (Skt. *klesha*)—and those that block us from buddhahood, the so-called knowledge (Skt. *jñeya*) obscurations.

30. The sadhana is the unpublished *The Glorious Guhyasamaja Self-Creation Yoga* (*Shri Guhyasamaja Atmotpatti Yoga*), usually known as the *Long Guhyasamaja Sadhana*, from the Tashi Lhunpo version arranged by Lama Tsongkhapa (trans. Tenzin Thurman, 1986).

31. The ten directions are the cardinal and ordinal directions plus up and down.

32. The five vajra dakinis are Shaptavajra, Rupavajra, Gandhavajra, Sparshavajra, and Rasavajra.

33. Generally, tantric deities are shown in sambhogakaya aspect, but in sadhanas such as this, during the practice of the taking death, intermediate state, and rebirth into the path as the three kayas, they are visualized as the simpler nirmanakaya aspect.

34. According to the Kalachakra system, the central channel is not inactive in the way the Guhyasamaja system explains, but all three channels contain different substances. See Daniel Cozort, *Highest Yoga Tantra* (Ithaca: Snow Lion Publications, 1986), p. 119.

35. The five branch winds arise from the life-supporting wind at the heart chakra and come and go by way of the five senses. They are the moving (or naga), the roving (or turtle), the perfectly flowing (or lizard), the intensely flowing (or devadatta), and the definitely flowing (or dhanamjaya) winds.

36. This chart is created from a commentary by Kyabje Trijang Rinpoche, *How to Do a Long Yamantaka Retreat*, published in Tibetan by Sera Mey Publishing House, 1999.

37. It is said that how long we are going to live depends on how much of this life-

supporting wind we have, which depends on our previous karma. We can actually calculate our lifespan from the rate of our breathing. There are certain practices in Vajrayana that use this wind to extend our life in order to complete the practices.

38. It would be neat to relate *bindu* or *tig-le* to the grosser drops and *bodhichitta* to the subtler, but it appears there is no such correlation.

39. This is according to the Guhyasamaja system. The Kalachakra system adds four other types of drops made from the red and white ones: the body drops located at the crown, the speech drops located at the throat and secret place, the mind drops located at the heart and center of the sexual organ, and the exalted wisdom drops located at the navel and tip of the sexual organ. See Cozort, *Highest Yoga Tantra*, p. 120.

40. Again, this is according to the Guhyasamaja system. In the Kalachakra system, the indestructible drop is not mentioned, the very subtle wind and mind abiding in the four types of drops. See Cozort, *Highest Yoga Tantra*, p. 120.

41. Tibetan Buddhism differentiates the diverse Buddhist philosophical views into four distinct schools: the two Hinayana schools of Vaibhashika (those who follow the Abhidharma text called the *Mahavibhasha*) and Sautrantika (those who follow the sutras) and the two Mahayana schools of Chittamatra (those who assert the reality of "mind only") and Madhyamaka (those who follow the "middle way" between eternalism and nihilism), which is further subdivided into Svatantrika (those who reason with autonomous syllogisms) and Prasangika (those who reason with logical consequences).

42. The Kalachakra tantra is slightly different. For an interesting comparison of Guhyasamaja and Kalachakra tantras, see Cozort, *Highest Yoga Tantra*, pp. 115–31. See also Kirti Tsenshap Rinpoche's *Principles of Buddhist Tantra* (Boston: Wisdom Publications, 2011).

43. From the viewpoint of highest yoga tantra, a sutra practitioner can only go so far. In order to complete the entire path, sooner or later, he or she will need to take on a tantric practice in order to refine the mind so that it can enter and dissolve into the heart chakra and hence attain enlightenment.

44. Lodoe, *Paths and Grounds of Guhyasamaja*, p. 51.

45. In other parts of his text he divides the completion stage into five, adding the generation stage and counting all the isolations as one. Chandrakirti's *Bright Lamp* is not translated into English, but Tsongkhapa's commentary, *Lamp to Illuminate the Five Stages*, which is based on Chandrakirti's, will soon have two English translations, including one by Gavin Kilty in *The Library of Tibetan Classics* (2012).

46. Modified from Lodoe, *Paths and Grounds of Guhyasamaja*, p. 53.

47. The twenty-five coarse objects of dissolution are: the four elements (earth, water, fire, wind), the five aggregates (form, feelings, discrimination, compositional factors, consciousness), the six sense sources (eye sense, ear sense, nose sense, tongue sense, body sense, mental sense), the five sense objects (colors and shapes, sounds, odors, tastes, tactile objects), and the five primordial wisdoms.

48. For a full explanation of *tumo*, see Glenn Mullin, *The Six Yogas of Naropa:*

Tsongkhapa's Commentary Entitled a Book of Three Inspirations (Ithaca: Snow Lion Publications, 2005), pp. 173–86. See also Lama Yeshe's *The Bliss of Inner Fire: Heart Practice of the Six Yogas of Naropa* (Boston: Wisdom Publications, 1998).

49. Modified from Lodoe, *Paths and Grounds of Guhyasamaja*, p. 54.

50. See note 35 above.

51. Modified from Lodoe, *Paths and Grounds of Guhyasamaja*, p. 59.

52. See Lodoe, *Paths and Grounds of Guhyasamaja*, pp. 97, 98.

53. Lodoe, *Paths and Grounds of Guhyasamaja*, p. 185.

54. Lodoe, *Paths and Grounds of Guhyasamaja*, p. 63.

55. Lodoe, *Paths and Grounds of Guhyasamaja*, pp. 73–74.

56. See note 29.

57. Modified from Cozort, *Highest Yoga Tantra*, p. 62.

GLOSSARY

ABHIDHARMA (Skt.): one of the three "baskets" of Buddhist scriptures, the one on metaphysics.

ACTUAL CLEAR LIGHT: the clear light that is without a trace of conceptuality, resulting from a direct realization of emptiness. It is contrasted with *simulated clear light*. *See also* clear light

ACTION SEAL (Skt. *karma mudra*): actual consort (as opposed to *wisdom seal*, a visualized consort).

AGGREGATES, THE FIVE (Skt. *pañcha skandha*): also "five heaps"; the traditional breakdown of a person's physical and mental constituents. They are form, feeling, discrimination, compositional factors, and consciousness.

ARHAT (Skt.): a practitioner who has achieved nirvana, or the cessation of personal suffering, in the Hinayana vehicle.

ARYA (Skt.): literally, a "superior" being; one who has gained a direct realization of emptiness in meditative equipoise during the path of seeing and has thereby uprooted the belief in self-existence.

AVALOKITESHVARA (Skt.; Tib. *Chenrezig*): the deity manifesting enlightened compassion.

BARDO (Tib.): the intermediate state of existence between death and rebirth.

BODHICHITTA (Skt.; Tib. *jangchub gyi sem*): the altruistic mind that seeks enlightenment in order to benefit all sentient beings. There are two types: *aspiring bodhichitta,* the mind that aspires to attain enlighten-ment, and *engaging bodhichitta,* the mind that actually engages in the bodhisattva's activities, such as the six perfections.

BODHICHITTA DROPS. *See* drops

CALM ABIDING (Skt. *shamatha;* Tib. *shi-ne*): a state of concentration in which the mind is able to abide steadily, without effort and for as long as desired, on an object of meditation.

CHAKRA (Skt.): a focal point of energy along the central channel; the main chakras are at the crown, throat, heart, navel, and sexual organ.

CHANNELS (Skt. *nadi;* Tib. *tsa*): the byways of the subtle body through which flow the various winds; of the 72,000, the main ones are the central channel (Skt. *avadhuti*), the right channel (Skt. *rasana*), and the left channel (Skt. *lalana*).

CLEAR LIGHT (Skt. *prabhasvara;* Tib. *osel*): the subtlest state of mind, which occurs naturally at the time of death or through the most advanced tantric practices. *See also* actual clear light; fundamental clear light; simulated clear light

CYCLIC EXISTENCE: samsara; the state of being constantly reborn into suf-fering due to delusion and karma.

DAKINI (Skt.; Tib. *khandroma*): literally "female sky-goer": a female being who helps arouse blissful energy in a qualified tantric practitioner.

DEITY YOGA: a meditation or yoga where the meditational deity is used, either as self-generation (where the meditator imagines him- or her-self as a deity) or as front-generation (where the deity is visualized in front).

DEITY: enlightened energy in the form of a being (such as Avalokitesh-vara), used as a tool in meditation.

DHARMADHATU (Skt.): Translated as either the "realm of phenomena" or the "realm of truth," the dharmadhatu is the purified mind in its nat-ural state.

DHARMAKAYA (Skt.): truth body; one of the two bodies achieved when the mind is completely purified and enlightenment is attained, the other being the rupakaya or form body; the result of the wisdom side of the practice.

DHYANI BUDDHAS (Skt.): the archetypal buddhas of the five buddha families, representing five primordial wisdoms; they are: Vairochana, Amitabha, Akshobhya, Ratnasambhava, and Amoghasiddhi.

DIVINE PRIDE (Tib. *lha'i ngagyal*): also called *divine identity*, the sense that one is the meditational deity.

DORJE (Tib.; Skt. *vajra*): meaning "indestructible," usually refers to small five-pronged ritual implement, symbolizing method and held in one hand with a bell symbolizing wisdom in the other. The term *vajra* is also used more broadly to indicate things related to the Vajrayana path.

DROPS (Skt. *bindu, tilaka*; Tib. *tig-le, jangsem*): one of the types of substances in the body, either white or red, coming from the indestructible drop and pervading the body. In the completion stage of tantra, the practitioner is able to cause the drops to melt and flow down the central channel, triggering great bliss.

EMANATION BODY. *See* nirmanakaya

EQUIPOISE. *See* meditative equipoise

FIVE AGGREGATES. *See* aggregates, the five

FIVE PATHS: the path of accumulation, preparation, meditation, seeing, and no more learning.

FIVE PRIMORDIAL WISDOMS (Skt. *pañchajñana*; Tib. *yeshe nga*): also called the five wisdoms; the basic energies in their purified form, relating to the five aggregates. They correspond to the five Dhyani Buddhas. They are: the mirror-like wisdom corresponding to Vairochana, the wisdom of analysis to Amitabha, the wisdom of equality to Ratnasambhava, the wisdom of achieving activities to Amoghasiddhi, and the dharmadhatu wisdom to Akshobhya.

FORM BODY. *See* rupakaya

FRONT-GENERATION: visualization of deity in front of oneself.

FUNDAMENTAL CLEAR LIGHT: the innate nature of the mind, carried by the subtlest wind, beyond all conceptuality.

GELUG (Tib.): founded by Lama Tsongkhapa, one of the four major traditions within Tibetan Buddhism. The others are Sakya, Nyingma, and Kagyu.

ILLUSORY BODY: body attained when winds dissolve in the indestructible drop at the heart.

IMPURE ILLUSORY BODY: illusory body obtained with a wisdom (visualized) consort, with still a trace of conceptualization.

INDIVIDUAL-LIBERATION PRACTITIONER: a practitioner of the Hinayana, who strives for personal liberation (as opposed to the universal liberation aspired to in the Mahayana).

KAPALA (Skt.; Tib. *töpa*): offering bowl made out of, or in the shape of, a human skull.

LAMRIM (Tib.): the "graduated path to enlightenment"; a way of presenting the Buddha's teachings in a systematic way. The genre is popular in the Gelug tradition.

LIFE FORCE (Skt. *prana*; Tib. *sogzin gyi lung*): the subtle wind that flows though the body in the psychic channels that is the vital, life-sustaining force, corresponding to the Chinese notion of *qi*.

MALA (Skt.): a rosary for counting mantras, usually consisting of 108 beads.

MANDALA (Skt.): the environment of the deity.

MANTRA (Skt.): literally, "that which holds"; usually a series of Sanskrit syllables connected with a particular deity practice that are recited over and over again. *Mantra* is also a synonym for tantra.

MANTRA GARLAND: the mantra made of light and standing around the rim of the moon disc during the visualization of the deity.

MEDITATIVE EQUIPOISE (Skt. *samahita*; Tib. *nyamzhag*): an undistracted state of mind that is achieved through various forms of meditation such as calm abiding and special insight, almost invariably referring to the realization of emptiness and contrasted to the post-meditative state.

MERIT FIELD: in tantra, this typically means the buddhas visualized during the preliminary practices of a sadhana.

MUDRA (Skt.): hand gesture.

NIRMANAKAYA (Skt.): the emanation body; of the two form bodies (*rupakaya*) of a buddha, this is the one that can be seen by ordinary beings.

NYUNGNÉ (Tib.): a two-day retreat on Thousand-Armed Avalokiteshvara involving fasting, prostrations, and silence.

PERFECTION VEHICLE: the Mahayana path from the sutras that is not Vajrayana.

PRANA. *See* life force

PRASANGIKA / PRASANGIKA-MADHYAMAKA (Skt.): the Middle Way Consequence school; the higher of the two subdivisions of Madhyamaka, the other being Svatantrika.

PRIMORDIAL LORD: Vajradhara, the most fundamental aspect of a tantric deity.

PRINCIPAL DEITY: the principal deity visualized (e.g., within a Guhyasamaja practice it would be Guhyasamaja).

PURE ILLUSORY BODY: illusory body obtained through using an action (actual) consort and hence without conceptualization.

REFUGE FIELD: visualization of buddhas done in the main part of the practice.

RUPAKAYA (Skt.): the form body; the body of a buddha that evolves from the winds (as opposed to the dharmakaya, which evolves from the mind).

SADHANA (Skt.): meditation manual.

SAMBHOGAKAYA (Skt.): the enjoyment body; of the two form bodies (*rupakaya*) of a buddha, this is the one that can only be seen by arya beings.

SAMSARA. *See* cyclic existence

SEAL (Skt. *mudra*). *See* action seal; wisdom seal

SEED SYLLABLE: In tantric visualizations, a Sanskrit syllable arising out of emptiness and from which in turn the meditation deity arises.

SELF-GENERATION: the visualization of oneself as a deity.

SHAMATHA (Skt.). *See* calm abiding

SIMULATED CLEAR LIGHT: the clear light achieved that still has a trace of conceptuality (as opposed to *actual* clear light, which comes from a direct realization of emptiness).

SPECIAL INSIGHT: (Skt. *vispashyana*) deep insight into a subject (usually emptiness) gained through meditation.

SPECIAL INSIGHT: the mind that conjoins with calm abiding to really know an object.

SUBTLE BODY: the network of channels, winds or energies, and drops within the coarse body.

SUBTLE DROPS. *See* drops

TRUTH BODY. *See* dharmakaya

WINDS (Skt. *vayu*; Tib. *lung*): the energy that runs through the channels of our subtle body and upon which ride our various consciousnesses. A major element of tantric practice is the manipulation of these winds during meditation.

WISDOM SEAL (Skt. *prajña mudra*): the visualized consort.

YIDAM (Tib.; Skt. *ishtadevata*): the main meditation deity used in a tantric practice.

BIBLIOGRAPHY

Asanga. *Abhidharmasamuccaya: The Compendium of the Higher Teaching.*
Trans. by Sara Boin-Webb of Walpola Rahula's French translation.
Fremont, CA: Asian Humanities Press, 2001.

Cozort, Daniel. *Highest Yoga Tantra.* Ithaca: Snow Lion Publications,
1986.

Dragpa, Panchen Sonam. *An Overview of Buddhist Tantra.* Dharamsala:
The Library of Tibetan Works and Archives, 1996.

FPMT, *Lama Chöpa Puja.* Portland, OR: FPMT.

Govinda, Lama Anagarika. *The Way of the White Clouds.* Boston:
Shambhala, 1988.

Gyatso, Tenzin, His Holiness the Dalai Lama. *The World of Tibetan Buddhism.* Trans. Thupten Jinpa. Boston: Wisdom Publications, 1995.

——, and Jeffrey Hopkins. *Kālachakra Tantra: Rite of Initiation.*
Boston: Wisdom Publications, 1999.

Kirti Tsenshap Rinpoché. *The Principles of Buddhist Tantra.* Trans. Ian
Coghlan and Voula Zarpani. Boston: Wisdom Publications, 2011.

Lati Rinbochay, and Jeffrey Hopkins. *Death, Intermediate State, and
Rebirth in Tibetan Buddhism.* Ithaca: Snow Lion Publications, 1979.

La Vallée Poussin, Louis de. *Abhidharmakośabhāsyam,* 4 vols. English
trans. by Leo Pruden. Berkeley, CA: Asian Humanities Press, 1991.

Lodoe, Yanchen Gawai. *Paths and Grounds of Guhyasamaja According to
Arya Nagarjuna.* Dharamsala: The Library of Tibetan Works and
Archives, 1995.

Losang Kälsang Gyatso, Seventh Dalai Lama. *Nyung Nä: The Means
of Achievement of the Eleven-Face Great Compassionate One*

(*Avalokiteśvara*) *of the* (*Bhikṣuṇī*) *Lakṣmī Tradition*. Boston: Wisdom Publications, 1995. Rev. ed., FPMT Education Services.

Mullin, Glenn. *The Six Yogas of Naropa: Tsongkhapa's Commentary Entitled a Book of Three Inspirations*. Ithaca: Snow Lion Publications, 2005.

Nagarjuna. *Nagarjuna's Precious Garland: Buddhist Advice for Living and Liberation*. Trans. and ed. by Jeffrey Hopkins. Ithaca: Snow Lion Publications, 1998.

Tsering, Geshe Tashi. *The Awakening Mind*. Boston: Wisdom Publications, 2008.

———. *The Four Noble Truths*. Boston: Wisdom Publications, 2005.

Tsongkhapa. *The Great Treatise on the Stages of the Path to Enlightenment* (Tib. *Lamrim Chenmo*), 3 vols. Trans. Lamrim Chenmo Translation Committee. Ithaca: Snow Lion Publications, 2000–2004.

———. *The Life and Teachings of Tsong Khapa*. Ed. by Robert A. F. Thurman. Dharamsala: Library of Tibetan Works and Archives, 1982.

———. *Tantric Ethics*. Trans. by Gareth Sparham. Boston: Wisdom Publications, 2005.

Vasubandhu. *Treasury of Higher Knowledge* (*Abhidharmakośa*). See La Vallée Poussin above.

———. *Exposition of the Treasury of Higher Knowledge* (*Abhidharmakośabhāṣyam*). See La Vallée Poussin above.

Yeshe, Lama Thubten. *The Bliss of Inner Fire: Heart Practice of the Six Yogas of Naropa*. Boston: Wisdom Publications, 1998.

———. *Introduction to Tantra*. Boston: Wisdom Publications, 1987.

Zopa Rinpoche, Lama Thubten. *The Heart of the Path*. Boston: Lama Yeshe Wisdom Archive, 2009.

INDEX

Tsongkhapa, 29, 43, 77, 147, 154
tumo. *See* inner heat practice
two obscurations. *See* obscuration
two truths, 13, 129

U
ultimate truth, 13, 129
union. *See* clear-light mind, union of
   the illusory body with

V
Vaibhashika school, 129
Vairochana, 96, 97, 98, 138
vajra, 105, 107
   and bell blessing, 93, 94
   and bell initiation, 36, 37, 38
   of great bliss and emptiness, 164
Vajra Garland Tantra, 28
vajra masters, 24–30, 36, 67
vajra repetition, 148–51
Vajradhara, 5, 17, 109, 134, 139, 140
Vajradhatvishvari, 109
Vajrasattva, 16, 51, 70–71, 94, 95,
   109
Vajrayana
   method and wisdom combined in,
      12–14
   names for, 5–9
   prerequisites for, 3–4
   refuge in, 3
   as resultant vehicle, 3
   unique features of, 9–14
vase breathing, 46, 47, 72, 73, 147
vase initiations, 35–39
Vasubandhu, 87
verbal isolation, 148–52
very subtle body and mind, 111–13,
   127
view, use of the term, 10
vipashyana. *See* special insight
vital wind. *See* prana
vows. *See* bodhisattva vows; individual libeartion vows; tantric vows

W
wang, 32, 71
water element, 84, 94
water initiation, 36, 37
Way of the White Clouds, The (Lama
   Govinda), 74–75
white appearance, 85, 86, 104
wind(s)
   black foods and, 42, 44
   death and, 81–82
   deity yoga and, 15
   enlightenment process and, 127
   the five main, 122–25
   with five rays of light, 157
   moving, into the central channel,
      79, 80, 82
   pranayama and, 71–74
   subduing, 46–48
   very subtle fundamental, 112–13
   vital (*prana*), 46, 122, 123–24
wind element, 84–85
wind vajra, 163
wisdom
   being, 68, 109
   initiation, 35, 38
   perfect control over, 90, 92
   seal (*prajña mudra*), 134, 155
   slight control of, 90, 91
   slight dawning of, 90, 91
withdrawal practice, 144
womb, 88–89, 126
word initiation, 35, 38

Y
Yangchen Gawai Lodoe, 79, 92, 148,
   153, 157, 159–60
Yeshe, Lama, 7, 21
yidam, 15–16. *See also* deities; deity
   yoga
yoga tantra, 36, 45, 48–59

Z
Zopa Rinpoche, Lama, 71

About the Authors

Geshe Tashi Tsering escaped Tibet in 1959 with his family at the age of one, and entered Sera Mey Monastic University in South India at thirteen, graduating sixteen years later as a Lharampa Geshe, the highest level. Requested by Lama Thubten Zopa Rinpoche, the spiritual director of the Foundation for the Preservation of the Mahayana Tradition (FPMT), to teach in the West, he became the resident teacher at Jamyang Buddhist Centre in London in 1994, where he developed *The Foundation of Buddhist Thought*, which has become one of the core courses in the FPMT's education program. He has taught the course in England and Europe since 1997.

Gordon McDougall was director of Cham Tse Ling, the FPMT's Hong Kong center, for two years in the 1980s and worked for Jamyang Buddhist Centre in London from 2000–2006. He has taken an active part in the development and administration of the *The Foundation of Buddhist Thought*.

THE FOUNDATION OF BUDDHIST THOUGHT

THE FOUNDATION OF BUDDHIST THOUGHT is a two-year course in Buddhist studies created by Geshe Tashi Tsering of Jamyang Buddhist Centre in London. The program draws upon the depth of Tibetan Buddhist philosophy to exemplify how Buddhism can make a real difference in the way we live our lives. *The Foundation of Buddhist Thought* is part of the Foundation for the Preservation of the Mahayana Tradition (FPMT) core study program. This course can be taken either in person or by correspondence. It consists of the following six four-month modules:

+ The Four Noble Truths
+ Relative Truth, Ultimate Truth
+ Buddhist Psychology
+ The Awakening Mind
+ Emptiness
+ Tantra

In addition to the related Wisdom book, each module includes approximately fifteen hours of professionally edited audio teachings on either CD or MP3 disc (or download), taken from Geshe Tashi's recent

London course. These are used in conjunction with guided meditations to explore each topic in depth. Each student is also part of a study group led by a tutor who facilitates discussions twice a month, helping the student to bring the topics to life through active dialogue with other members of the group. Essays and exams are also an essential part of the curriculum. This mixture of reading, listening, meditating, discussing, and writing ensures that each student will gain an understanding and mastery of these profound and important concepts.

A vital aspect of the course is Geshe Tashi's emphasis on the way these topics affect our everyday lives. Even a philosophical topic such as relative and ultimate truth is studied from the perspective of the choices we make on a daily basis, and the way to begin to develop a more realistic approach to living according to the principles of Buddhist thought.

"A real life-changer. The jigsaw that was Dharma all suddenly fits into place."—*course graduate*

To find out more about *The Foundation of Buddhist Thought*, please visit our website at **www.buddhistthought.org**. To find out more about FPMT study programs, please visit **www.fpmt.org**.

About Wisdom Publications